AFRICA OVERLAND

DEDICATION

To all the great many friends I have met in Africa that are involved in the overland industry... they are a unique, entertaining and genuine bunch of people.

AFRICA OVERLAND

Lizzie Williams

First published in 2005 by Struik Publishers
(a division of New Holland Publishing)
(South Africa) (Pty) Ltd)
New Holland Publishing is a member of Johnnic Communications Ltd

London • Cape Town • Sydney • Auckland

Cornelis Struik House, 80 McKenzie Street, Cape Town 8001

ISBN 1 77007 187 3

1 3 5 7 9 10 8 6 4 2

Publishing Manager: Dominique le Roux
Managing Editor: Lesley Hay-Whitton
Designer: Martin Jones
Editors: Christine Didcott and Michelle Coburn
Proofreader: Helen de Villiers
Indexer: Mary Lennox

Reproduction by Hirt & Carter Cape (Pty) Ltd
Printed and bound by Kyodo Printing Co (S'pore) Pte Ltd, Singapore

Visit us at www.struik.co.za

Log on to our photographic website www.imagesofafrica.co.za for an African experience.

CONTENTS

ABOUT THE AUTHOR

Lizzie has travelled extensively as an independent overlander and has visited 20 African countries in total. She has worked as a tour leader on overland trucks for four years and has led numerous overland tours throughout eastern and southern Africa. She regularly writes and compiles brochures for the overlanding companies specialising in African travel. She writes guidebooks for Footprint and has written these guides for South Africa, Kenya and Tanzania. Future projects include updating the *Footprint Guide to Namibia*, as well as writing a new book on Zambia. She has updated the *Rough Guide to Turkey* and has written the first guidebook on Nigeria for Bradt.

Note: Apart from the websites recommended on p304, the official tourism websites for each country are good places for up to date information on weather conditions, accommodation and useful links to other informative websites. Visit the following official sites: Kenya: *www.magicalkenya.com*; Uganda: *www.visituganda.com*; Tanzania: *www.tanzaniatouristboard.com*; Malawi: *www.tourismmalawi.com*; Zambia: *www.zambiatourism.com*; Zimbabwe: *www.zimbabwetourism.co.zw*; Botswana: *www.botswana-tourism.gov.bw*; Namibia: *www.met.gov.na*; South Africa: *www.satourism.net*.

AUTHOR'S PREFACE

It's fair to say that I've done a lot of travelling in Africa over the last few years. I've experienced minibus safaris in the Ngorongoro Crater and on the Serengeti plains; I've swum with a horse in Lake Malawi and stroked a cheetah in Namibia; I've slept in a rondavel on the slopes of a volcano in Uganda and in a washed-out tent in a storm in Botswana; I've watched the sun rise over Mozambique's tropical islands and seen it sink over the biggest sand dunes in the world in Namibia; I've plummeted off Vic Falls Bridge on a bungee jump and ridden an elephant through the Zambian bush; I've riverboarded down the Zambezi and stared into the soft brown eyes of a gorilla in Uganda.

You might think that all of this could only be experienced by a 'lucky' travel writer. But you'd be wrong – this could be your story too, as these are just some of the highlights of an overland trip between Kenya and Cape Town. I was lucky enough to work as a tour leader on overland trucks for four-and-half years, and took hundreds of passengers through Africa's alluring destinations.

For anyone who thinks that overlanding is all about being cooped up in a rickety old truck with a bunch of intolerable passengers, think again. Overlanding can turn out to be the trip of a lifetime, and even the most die-hard backpackers and independent travellers can benefit from joining a tour on an overland truck. The main advantages of overlanding are: the ability to cover large areas in a limited time; the security of knowing that you have somewhere safe to sleep each night – even if it's in a tent in the middle of nowhere; safety in numbers and the companionship of a large group; not having to organise your own guides or transport for spin-off activities. But, if you feel group overlanding is not for you, then those who have more time and money can organise their own trip in their own vehicle, be it a car, motorbike or even a bicycle. This gives you the ultimate freedom to explore Africa as you want to, and many hundreds of independent expeditions cross Africa each year.

Whichever way you choose to travel, an overland trip through Africa is memorable, educational, and – above all – lots of fun. I hope this book will be a wonderful souvenir for anyone who has been lucky enough to have travelled through Africa by road, and seen and done all the amazing things this fantastic continent offers. Get packing, and enjoy the ride…

INTRODUCTION

Africa is a continent of mystery and excitement; of diverse cultures, big game and thrilling activities; of natural wonders, vast wilderness areas and memorable experiences. It is a destination filled with breathtaking scenery, from high mountains and tropical rainforests, to fertile plains and spectacular deserts. The continent offers many rewarding wildlife encounters: gorillas and chimpanzees live in the misty jungles, and the famous Big Five teem on the vast, open plains. Her sheer size (the second largest continent on earth), number of countries (54), and high population (800 million), make deciding where to begin exploring seem an overwhelming task, especially when difficulties such as language barriers, political upheavals and health risks are considered. But, despite these factors, most countries are safe, rewarding places in which to travel.

The best way to discover the African continent is by travelling overland, whether it is in your own fully-equipped vehicle or on a tour with one of the commercial overland truck companies (*see acknowledgements, p304*). The term 'overlanding' became a firm fixture of travel-lore in the late 1960s and was originally coined to describe a group of people – ranging from a convoy to a single vehicle – who drove across Africa or Asia. It is self-sufficient travel in a 4x4 vehicle, purpose-built truck, motorbike or even bicycle, when all the equipment for camping, cooking, and maintaining the vehicle is carried with you. This is the most economical and convenient way of getting off the beaten track and moving from country to country. The desire to go just where you want to, and personally face the challenge of crossing jungle or desert, rewards every overlander with a very personal and memorable trip. Nothing is certain in Africa and you never know exactly what lies ahead – that is what makes overlanding here so special. It can be the trip of a lifetime, filled with exciting wildlife moments, thrilling adventure activities, campfire camaraderie, and memorable nights camping under the enormous African sky.

The continent's tracks and roads cross the wild side of Africa, taking you to meet the people and experience local conditions. Overlanding puts money straight into the local economy and directly benefits the people of Africa – rather than tour operators based elsewhere in the world. This form of travel assists the resident communities of host countries, as overlanders shop in local markets, eat in small restaurants, use local guides and safari operators, and stay in campsites staffed by local people. The World Bank estimates that as little as ten percent of tourist expenditure worldwide actually ends up in the country of destination, but a study by Greenwich University in the United Kingdom showed that the figure for overlanding operations was as high as 56 percent.

2

Page 8
Overland vehicles can take full advantage of Africa's wide spaces.

This Page
1 Crossing the Tropic of Cancer in the Northern Hemisphere.
2 Early overlanders had to cope with broken bridges and barely-there roads.

But, overlanding is not for everyone. It requires patience, a willingness to pitch in, and a good sense of humour. This form of travel does involve a bit more hard work than the conventional package holiday or African safari – you must be prepared to get stuck in, participate, cook, put up a tent each night, maintain the vehicle, source food and water, and drive over long distances on roads that are sometimes appalling. But, there is no better way to experience the rhythm and soul of Africa. If you can you see yourself sitting around a campfire with a warm Tanzanian beer under a canopy of stars, or peeling potatoes for 20 people, or laughing out loud when a torrential downpour floods your tent in the middle of the night, then you could be a potential overlander. This can never be described as a luxury holiday – it's much more fun than that!

The epic overland trip from Europe to Cape Town has been well travelled over the last 100 years. During the colonial era, settlers travelled from Europe in vehicles laden with their worldly possessions hoping to start a new life on the African plains. The Automobile Association of South Africa published a route book in 1949 titled *Trans-African Highways – A Route Book of the Main Trunk Roads in Africa*, listing mileage and directions for many varied trans-continental routes. It also gave advice on equipment, vehicles and paperwork needed. Back then, travelling across the continent could be accomplished relatively easily in political terms, though, with few roads, facilities, or even maps, driving from the top of Africa to the bottom was an arduous task.

These pioneers were followed in the 1960s by hardy young adventurers in 4x4s who wanted to complete the Cairo to Cape Town route, and painstakingly eased their vehicles across deserts, through steamy jungles, and along barely-there roads. In the 1970s and 1980s truck tours became popular and a number of commercial overland companies were established. These first truck tours took many months and could, depending on vehicles and preparation, be very strenuous – passengers were often called upon to push the truck out of mud or sand, or help with changing tyres.

In the early days, the concept was simple and cheap: bolt some coach seats into a second-hand army truck, stock it with spares, tents and food, sign up some punters and hit the road. Early itineraries were loose, if they existed at all, and expeditions developed according to the interests and input of their participants. Several months later, despite having had to negotiate broken bridges, mechanical breakdowns and bureaucratic disasters, 20 weary but enlightened overlanders would eventually gaze upon Table Mountain.

To this day, Africa provides overlanders with the greatest motoring challenge available in the world. There are inevitably a number of key decisions to be made before embarking on such a trip: where to go, who to go with, how to pay for it, and the last and most difficult – making that decision to leave everything behind and go for it.

There are many commercial overland operators offering a bewildering assortment of itineraries and routes. They all have decades of experience behind them and many of the owner-operators

"Twenty years from now you will be more disappointed by the things you didn't do than by the ones you did do. So throw off the bowlines, sail away from the safe harbour. Catch the trade winds in your sails. Explore. Dream. Discover." – Mark Twain

were among the first independent overlanders who pioneered the early routes through Africa.

The basic philosophy of involvement and participation on tour survives intact. However, just as Africa and the nature of African tourism have evolved, so has overlanding. As clientele and expectations have changed, overlanding has matured. Today's overland passengers still expect to pitch their own tent, but they also want a reliable vehicle, a well-trained and capable crew, and logistical back-up. Over the years, vehicles and routes have constantly improved: vehicle design is better (bearing passenger comfort in mind) and infrastructure across Africa has improved. Where once overland groups would camp in the bush each night, today

there is a wide range of excellent campsites catering for overlanders and their vehicles, many with a range of activities, bars, restaurants and good facilities. On the Kenya to Cape route (*see p14*), it is now possible to stay in a secure campsite every night, and there are few times when a shower or a beer are not available – whether they will be hot or cold respectively is another matter altogether!

Over the decades, the general state of the roads has steadily improved. Only a few years ago it would take several days to negotiate potholed roads and washed-away bridges in a 4x4 to get between destinations, and border crossings were riddled with reputedly corrupt or suspicious officials. Today, many of the tracks have become tarred highways, and where it once took weeks to drive a few hundred kilometres, it now only takes a couple of days. More than 85 percent of the main roads between Morocco and Cape Town are now tar-sealed. Overland trips have therefore become much quicker and it's feasible for people to explore considerable parts of Africa in only a few weeks. Some trips are shorter and more modular – you can take a small bite out of a much bigger journey. And there are a number of softer options, which explains why the average age of overlanders is

1–4 Getting off the beaten track can be arduous because of rough roads, but experiencing the isolation of the African bush makes it all worthwhile.

increasing, and some bring their young families along too. Thanks to a comprehensive range of trips and excellent flight links between Africa and the rest of the world, you can discover the wonders of the continent on an overland tour that can last anywhere from a week to a few months.

Then there are those who do it themselves. Every year hundreds of independent overlanders throw their jobs in, close up their homes, and depart from Europe or South Africa to cross Africa in their own fully-equipped vehicles, motorbikes and even bicycles. Driving your own vehicle gives you the flexibility and freedom to go exactly where you want to, and to take as long about it as you wish. Nothing matches the achievement of crossing miles and miles of Africa on a journey that can change your life, and there is no better way to get to know more about your own personal capabilities. Some take a year or two to complete the epic journey, and others love it so much that they turn around and drive all the way back again.

5&6 Vehicles can get stuck and bogged in deep sand or mud. A vital piece of equipment to carry is a sand ladder that provides traction for the wheels to get out of a hole or ditch.

7 Some of Africa's roads today are tarred super-highways.

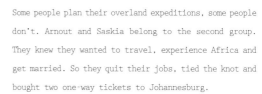

Some people plan their overland expeditions, some people don't. Arnout and Saskia belong to the second group. They knew they wanted to travel, experience Africa and get married. So they quit their jobs, tied the knot and bought two one-way tickets to Johannesburg.

The couple bought a car as soon as they arrived in South Africa, and within two weeks they were fully equipped for their trip. They ended up travelling overland all the way back to Amsterdam - 46 000 kilometres that took them a little over a year.

They knew nothing about cars when they started out, but they've learnt - the hard way. A broken fan in the middle of the desert; broken bearings, brakes and clutch - no one can tell them anything they don't already know!

Africa wasn't their first time on a long trip. They 'did' Cairo to Sulawesi (Indonesia) by public transport a few years back, but Africa stole their hearts. Great beaches in Mozambique, amazing landscapes in South Africa, the colours of the desert in Namibia, the plains of the Serengeti, and the mountain gorillas in Rwanda - each of them were very special highlights.

People sometimes ask the couple, 'Isn't it difficult to do a trip like this?'

They always answer, 'All you have to do is quit your job, buy a car and start driving, and the rest will follow. The best thing about Africa is its beautiful people. Everyone thinks civilisation stops beyond the borders of South Africa, but everywhere on the continent we felt the enormous hospitality and friendliness of the people. Other things that made this trip very special: the wide open spaces, the inventiveness of the African mechanics, and life in the bush.

Back in their tiny Amsterdam apartment, the thing they miss the most is having a *braai* on their own wood fire, with a glass of excellent South African wine.

Arnout Hemel & Saskia de Jongh

Classic Kenya to the Cape

Overland trips can last anywhere from a few days, to a whole year or more, and can run the whole length of Africa from Morocco to Cape Town. The most popular region for overlanding, however, is East and southern Africa from Kenya to Cape Town, in either direction. This route has become an alluring expedition for many travellers. It's the most accessible part of Africa, all the commercial operators offer trips on this route, and even those doing a complete Trans-Africa overland will find themselves between Kenya and the Cape on part of their journey.

Beginning in Nairobi, this classic trip covers East and southern Africa, taking in Kenya, Uganda, Tanzania, Malawi, Zambia, Zimbabwe, Botswana, Namibia, and ending in South Africa. Each of these countries is covered in its own chapter in this book (*see contents for chapter details, and map on inside front flap*).

You'll find that between Lake Victoria and Table Bay, there are seemingly endless game parks, beaches, deserts and wetlands waiting to be explored. Highlights of the trip include enjoying an encounter with a gentle ape in Uganda's misty mountains, watching the Zambezi River tumble over the Victoria Falls, viewing the shimmering dunes and deserts of the ancient Namib, spotting the Big Five on the endless plains in the national parks and game reserves, and meeting diverse people – from red-robed Masai warriors in Kenya, to the warm-hearted people of Malawi.

1–5 The route between Kenya and the Cape passes through a variety of ever changing landscapes.

Most trips head west from Nairobi across the floor of the Rift Valley along the main Mombasa–Kampala road that forms part of the Trans-Africa Highway. In this region there is the option to visit the Masai Mara Game Reserve to the south on the border with Tanzania, or some of the Rift Valley lakes such as Lake Nakuru or Lake Naivasha. The road continues over the border into Uganda and, after crossing the Nile, enters the capital Kampala. It then heads across the equator to the southwestern town of Kabale, where you will find the forests where the mountain gorillas live. The region

around the Virunga Volcanoes, which straddle southwest Uganda, Rwanda and the Democratic Republic of Congo, is the only place in the world where the rare mountain gorillas live and they can be seen on a popular gorilla trek.

Independent overlanders could also take in some of Uganda's national parks further to the north. The usual route from Uganda back into Kenya is along the same route that goes back via Kampala and Jinja to the Kenyan border.

There is effectively one road that links Nairobi with Cape Town. Most overland tours head south into Tanzania to the safari capital, Arusha. From here, there is the option to visit East Africa's greatest game parks, the Serengeti and the Ngorongoro Crater. A super-highway, which passes the foot of Africa's tallest mountain, Kilimanjaro, now links Arusha with Dar es Salaam further to the south on the Tanzanian coast. Dar es Salaam is the departure point for ferry trips to the exotic island of Zanzibar, and overland vehicles can be parked safely at the city's campsites for a few days.

The main road continues south from Dar es Salaam, through rural Tanzania, to Malawi, a sliver of a country dominated by the freshwater Lake Malawi. Once across the border, the roads deteriorate slightly but there is access to the entire western shore of the lake, where there are many resorts. From Malawi's capital Lilongwe, another road heads south and crosses the entire country of Zambia. Stops en route through Zambia include the South Luangwa National Park and the capital city of Lusaka. To the north of this road, an alternative route, referred to as the Great North Road, runs from the Tanzania border parallel with the Lilongwe to Lusaka road to the south.

All overlanders end up at the Victoria Falls, one of the highlights of any trip through Africa. The spectacular falls can be visited from the Zambian town of Livingstone, or from the town of Victoria Falls on the Zimbabwean side. From both towns, the Botswana border is less than 100 kilometres away, to the west, along the Zambezi River.

Once in Botswana, the first highlight is the Chobe National Park where there is the option of going on organised safaris, both by 4x4 and by boat on the Chobe River. Further south is the delicate ecosystem of the Okavango Delta. Overland vehicles can park up in the town of Maun at the edge of the delta, while overlanders explore the pristine delta by foot and *mokoro* (dug-out canoe).

From Maun, there are two routes into Namibia. The first crosses the northern fringes of the Kalahari Desert – on what is part of the Trans-Kalahari Highway – to Namibia's capital of Windhoek. The second route heads north from Maun and enters Namibia at the Caprivi Strip. From both directions, it's easy enough to explore the highlights of northern Namibia. These include Kaokoland, with its desolate scenery and intriguing tribespeople, Damaraland's ancient rock paintings and desert elephants, and the game-filled waterholes of the Etosha National Park.

Further south is the Skeleton Coast Park, where thousands of seals can be seen at Cape Cross. The coastal resort of Swakopmund also warrants at least a few days to enjoy the many adventure activities on offer, including exploring the dune fields that surround the town.

6 Joining an overland truck is about sharing your travelling experiences as a group.
7 Independent overlanders have the freedom to go where they wish.

More sand can be seen further south in the Namib-Naukluft Park, home to the biggest dunes in the world around Sossusvlei. The highlight here is driving into the park to watch a dramatic sunrise or sunset, when the colour of the sand turns to a deep orange. Further south is the quirky fishing town of Lüderitz, where the adjacent ghost town of Kolmanskop is a memorial to the history of the region's diamond mining industry.

Just to the north of the border with South Africa is the dramatic Fish River Canyon, the largest canyon in Africa. The Orange River marks the border between Namibia and South Africa, and here there is the opportunity to canoe on the river between the two countries.

On the last leg of this epic, 12 000-kilometre journey, the N7 runs down the entire western side of South Africa to Cape Town. There are a number of small country towns en route to break the journey to the 'Mother City'.

Adrenalin highs

This Spread
1 Lifelong friends can be made on overland truck trips.
2 Having a good attitude means that everyone will get along.

Africa is one of the world's leading adventure destinations and the Kenya–Cape route offers numerous exciting activities, allowing you to discover the continent from new, extraordinary angles. Some of the adrenalin highs include hot-air ballooning over the Masai Mara in Kenya or the Serengeti in Tanzania; white-water rafting or riverboarding on the Nile in Uganda, or the Zambezi River between Zambia and Zimbabwe; quad-biking along the Nile in Uganda or through the dunes in Namibia; and scenic flights over the Okavango Delta, the Namib Desert or Victoria Falls. Then there's bungee jumping over the Nile or into the Zambezi Gorge; sand-boarding down Namibia's dunes; watching elephants from a boat cruise on the Zambezi or Chobe rivers; riding elephants through the Zambian bush; tracking wild dog by foot in the Okavango Delta; or sky-diving over the Namibian desert.

The Big Five

Africa's wildlife is its biggest drawcard and travelling overland affords excellent opportunities to visit the continent's magnificent national parks. The Big Five (the collective name for lion, leopard, elephant, buffalo and rhino), are the most popular animals amongst travellers, due to their size, rarity and the sheer excitement of spotting them in the wild. Few people know that they were given the 'Big Five' tag by hunters in the early twentieth century, who identified these animals as the most difficult to hunt. Nowadays, hunting is strictly controlled and the Big Five, as well as the many other equally interesting species, are protected in reserves like the Ngorongoro Crater, Serengeti National Park, Masai Mara Game Reserve, the Okavango Delta and the Chobe and Etosha national parks.

A truckin' good time

Every year hundreds of overland trucks explore the African continent (and beyond), carrying groups of up to 30 overlanders on an adventure they're unlikely to forget. Journeying in an overland truck with one of the many commercial operators is the cheapest way to see Africa, and the ideal choice if you're short of time and are the kind of person who likes to explore in a group with like-minded, enthusiastic, fun-loving people. It's the kind of adventure on which you have to be willing to get your hands dirty and participate as part of a team. The vehicles are fitted out with everything you need, as well as comfortable seats and large windows to give you the ideal vantage point to view the sights of Africa.

However, although they are organised tours, these trips do not have the same level of routine or luxury as a package holiday. Realistically, group travel can also get claustrophobic at times, especially when personalities clash. But, if you set off with the right attitude, this is undoubtedly the best way to meet new people and cram countless fantastic experiences into a relatively short period of time.

The tours are run according to an organised itinerary, including set departure and arrival dates, and are led by a tour leader and driver/mechanic. One of the main advantages of booking a truck trip is that all the planning and preparation is done by the overland company. The company will brief you in good time on what you have to organise before you leave home, such as vaccinations and travel insurance, and will advise on what you should pack for the trip. After that, all you have to do is turn up at the departure point and wait for the fun to begin.

The experienced crew are familiar with the route, know where to camp each night and know how long it takes to get there – all making the journey faster and more efficient than it would be for independent travellers. An added bonus is that the leaders are accustomed to liaising with border crossings and African bureaucracy, meaning that trucks tend to have fewer problems when dealing with officials than do independent travellers, who might be facing these situations for the first time.

The majority of overland travellers are between 20 and 50 years old, although commercial overland tours also attract anyone from teenagers on 'gap' years, to older people who want to travel

3–5 A good vehicle design and regular mechanical maintenance contribute to the smooth running of an overland tour.

in their retirement. It's not about age, but rather about attitude – flexible, easy-going people with a certain amount of team spirit are most suited to this form of travel. And, while you do not need to be super-fit, you do need to be able to climb in and out of the vehicle, pitch your own tent and carry equipment. People of all nationalities join overland tours, some join trips together with a partner or group of friends, but many travel on their own. Group sizes normally range from between six and 27, depending on what type of vehicle is used.

A phenomenal amount of work and planning goes into the design of the perfect overland vehicle. It must be reliable and easy to maintain, and capable of transporting its occupants over any type of terrain in relative comfort. It also needs to be equipped as a travelling home for the duration of the trip. Commercial overland companies use purpose-built trucks, designed to carry everything needed for the trip on-board.

In the early years of commercial overlanding, ex-military vehicles tended to be popular. In the United Kingdom, old army Bedfords were often revamped into overland trucks, whilst the German soft-top military MAN trucks – indestructible vehicles looking almost like gigantic 4x4s – made the ultimate overlanding machines. These days, the majority of overland trucks are Mercedes, which tend to require the least number of modifications to their running gear and suspension before an expedition. This is also one of the more popular brands of truck in Africa, meaning that the availability of spares locally can be a major help if anything goes wrong. Leyland, Scania or DAF trucks are also widely used.

The trucks usually begin life on the assembly lines as flat-bed trucks, before the overland operators or coach-builders fit them with backs, enabling the vehicle to carry luggage, people and equipment safely. There are various designs, but the trucks generally have roll-up sides or windows that slide across for game viewing and photography; a fridge or cool box;

They're often expected to be not only drivers and tour leaders, but also diplomats, ambassadors, accountants, motivators, social workers and, occasionally, marriage-guidance counsellors too. To top it all, they must also be qualified mechanics and first-aiders.

It's also important for overland travellers to remember what the crew are not. Rather than being guides, they are leaders. They are not historians, geologists, or tropical disease experts, but rather experts in steering the group through otherwise unfamiliar territory. They can't identify every single mammal, bird, insect and plant in Africa – specialist guides with that depth of knowledge work only for the most exclusive, most expensive safari companies. Instead, overland crew have extensive knowledge about how to get their passengers safely from one end of Africa to the other in a relaxed and enjoyable way. They are personable, keen and conscientious, and have great passion for the countries they are taking people through.

The drivers are not only responsible for transporting passengers safely from A to B, but also for mechanical maintenance. They service the truck, changes tyres, parts, and filters, and generally know what to do if something goes wrong, especially when the truck breaks down in the middle of nowhere, or when it gets stuck in mud or sand. Drivers have a proven ability to maintain and fix things on their own – because who's to say there is going to be a convenient garage or workshop nearby.

It's the tour leader's job to organise everything en route and ensure that the whole trip runs smoothly. They are responsible for providing the group with food and shelter, giving brief information about the areas they are travelling through, and organising optional excursions and activities. They do the accounts and additional paperwork, and supervise the group when crossing borders or obtaining visas.

1 Truck interiors are designed to be comfortable and sociable.
2 Each truck has an easily accessible kitchen.
3 Trucks are designed for all terrains.
4 Trucks have large windows or roll-up sides for game viewing and photography.

a stereo; comfortable inward-, forward- or backward-facing coach seats; lockers for use during the day; interior and exterior lighting; gas cooker; fire grate; and ample storage space for luggage, tents, camping stools, food and cooking equipment. In addition to this, the truck carries drinking water in either a tank or jerry cans, spare tyres, parts and tools, and – in a concealed place in the truck – is a secure, lockable box that's used as a safe.

The crew

The truck companies employ overland crew to lead and drive their trips, and some also employ a safari cook. The crew work very hard in a 24-hour, seven-day a week job – and they love it.

'I went on my own and met up with 15 other people. We camped the whole way and mostly made our own meals. This trip convinced me that using an overland company is the best way to see Africa cheaply if you don't mind camping and roughing it, have limited time, and are willing to share in various duties. I'm normally an independent traveller and abhor anything that smacks of being organised, but when you have to be back at a job eight weeks down the road and want to fit in as much as possible, especially when spending megabucks on airfare, this is a good compromise.

At the start I felt I would never remember everyone's names, what job I had volunteered for and how to do it, and how many vegetarians there were when I was on cooking duty. But it was amazing how quickly we got to know each other once on the back of the truck. I was very lucky to have an awesome group.

At times the trip was a lot of hard work - we were up at the crack of dawn, or earlier on some days, and every day was jam-packed with driving or excursions. Nevertheless, we had an absolute blast. We saw and did so much in just a few short weeks, and it was brilliant to share everything with the rest of the group.

Our truck and equipment were in good condition, the trip leader was very capable, and the overland company provided unfailing backup when it was needed. Each night, over dinner around the campfire, the trip leader would tell us what to expect the next day - where and how far we were going, what we could do, and practical things, like if we'd have the opportunity to change money, or go to a market to buy food.

I had never slept in a tent before, but my tent buddy and I soon got used to pitching our tent and it was exciting falling asleep to the sounds of Africa - even if the ground was hard at times. The seats on the truck were comfortable, even on the very long driving days, and we decided to keep swapping seats each day so that we were always sitting next to someone different.

Everyone in the group was good-spirited and game for anything. I've kept in touch with about half of them - three of us are even thinking of doing another overland trip next year to somewhere else.'
Jennifer Franklyn

"The journey, not the arrival, matters."
– T.S. Eliot

5 By carrying all equipment and supplies, trucks are completely self-sufficient.
6 Vehicles are custom-built specifically for African overland tours.

"One's destination is never a place, but a new way of seeing things."
— Henry Miller

Going solo

Independent overlanders are of all ages and come from all walks of life. What they have in common is the dream of putting their ordinary lives on hold, and driving across Africa on an unforgettable journey of discovery.

Independent journeys require a lot of careful preparation. Buying the right vehicle and equipment takes time and money, routes need to be thoroughly researched, and becoming familiar with basic mechanics and off-road driving technique is highly advisable.

The planning process can be great fun – spreading your map of Africa out on the kitchen table at home beforehand is all part of the overland experience. Whatever type of preparation is needed, from customising the vehicle and buying equipment, to health practicalities and tying up loose ends at home, plenty of time should be allowed – many people take a few years to plan their trips. Good preparation means avoiding potential disasters later. Crossing the Sahara Desert without enough fuel or water, without a proper map and compass, or spare parts and the skills to match, could prove to be a deadly mistake.

Overland tour operators have a wealth of knowledge and, even with that experience, they are not going to set off with a battered old truck bought only a week before. The same applies to your own vehicle. The Africa Overland Network (*www.africa-overland.net*) website is an invaluable resource, both for inspiration and for giving essential information. It links over 200 websites documenting past and present Africa overland trips. The great thing about overlanders is that they love making lists and sharing information. Most websites therefore have detailed equipment and spares lists, descriptions of vehicle modifications, and plenty of helpful tips and advice.

Your route is bound to change once you are on the road, because you will meet other people on the way who will have useful tips on what to see and do, and in which direction you should be heading.

1 There is no such thing as too much preparation.
2 A little mechanical know-how is essential.

3 Planning the route is an exciting part of the adventure.
4 Careful planning on what to take is important when you are riding something as small as a scooter.

But, for budget and timing purposes, you will need to plan some sort of vague route before you set off. Start by writing down a list of places you would like to visit, and then research the climatic and political features of these areas that will determine when, and for how long, you will visit. Allow plenty of time: an independent overland trip is not just about driving from point A to B, but more about seeing the continent and meeting the people. A great advantage of being an independent overlander is having the freedom to find a beautiful beach, fall in love with it, and set up camp for a week, instead of having to move on the next day.

Even if you have very little mechanical knowledge, you can still go on your own overland trip, but the quality of your vehicle to begin with will be even more important. Independent overlanders have the choice of either buying – from someone who has previously done a trip – something that's already been adapted into an overland vehicle, or completely revamping a new one for themselves.

"A great advantage of being an independent overlander is having the freedom to find a beautiful beach, fall in love with it, and set up camp for a week, instead of having to move on the next day."

Opinion is divided on which is the best overland vehicle for independent travellers, but the choice really comes down to the Toyota Land Cruiser and Land Rover. Both are commonly used in Africa, making spare parts easier to find. Factors in the decision about which of the two to choose include reliability, personal preference, cost and, crucially, the ability to maintain it yourself. You'll need to carry essential spares, a full tool kit and a workshop repair manual. You should also research what type of mechanical problems you're likely to experience and how to sort them out.

How the finished vehicle will look depends on how you choose to put it together, as well as what equipment you want to take on the trip and how you'd like to attach it to your vehicle. Unless it's carefully put together, Africa's roads will shake it to bits. Simple, strong and practical are the key words to think about when equipping an overland vehicle. You'll need to carry similar equipment to that of an overland truck, but on a smaller scale. A roof tent is a good idea, long-range fuel tanks, adequate water storage, and comfortable seats for the rough roads are important. Secure storage for equipment is also essential, as things have a habit of going missing unless they are under lock and key. Those travelling by motorbike or bicycle are especially limited in what they can carry, and space is often restricted to custom-designed panniers fitted to the back of the bike.

'We are in the middle of our eight-month overland trip through eastern and southern Africa. We started in Cape Town and our goal is to circle Lake Victoria and then return to Cape Town via a different route. Because we're in Uganda, it means we're almost on the return leg - unfortunately!

You can choose between many overland routes and, without a doubt, any route you take is going to be fantastic. The fun starts before you even depart, when you start planning the route and preparing the car. When you read about all those interesting places, you can hardly believe you're actually going to see them - if the car keeps working, if you don't get sick, if nothing happens back home. Naturally, the most interesting experiences will be the parts you didn't plan. Adventure is what you're hoping for.

Travelling through southern and East Africa is much easier than people think. Sure, it's the 'real' Africa and you'll have to deal with some unusual situations. But, with a little bit of common sense, it's not hard to find money, fuel, food and safe places to sleep. Nothing bad has happened so far, and we consider Africa a safe destination. This part of Africa is varied, rugged and very beautiful, with nice people and the best opportunities to see the greatest wildlife on our planet. And anybody can do it.

We will never forget the pleasure and convenience of being able to drive thousands of kilometres through Africa in our own reliable Land Cruiser. We have the ultimate feeling of independence - we know our vehicle can take us anywhere and, with our rooftop tent (there's no better place to sleep!), fridge and the right camping equipment, we are completely self-sufficient.

We especially loved the ever-changing scenery. It started with the dry Namib Desert - Kaokoland and Damaraland were

absolute highlights because of the wonderful Himba and Herero people. Then there was the incredible wildlife in Etosha and the Okavango Delta.

Zambia also has really special people. We loved the way it slowly became greener as we moved north and before we knew it, we'd reached the tropical rainforests of Rwanda and Uganda. Living on the slopes of the volcanoes in Rwanda, Uganda and Congo are the famous mountain gorillas. It's easy to organise a trip to see them - quite expensive but worth every penny. Also, the chimpanzee treks we made in Tanzania, Rwanda and Uganda were top of the bill.

Next, we are looking forward to seeing the wildlife in the world-famous national parks further south, and meeting the tribespeople and relaxing on the white beaches of the Indian Ocean in Kenya, Tanzania and Mozambique. What a way of life!'

Coen & Jeanette Zijlstra

1–5 Independent overlanders travel in a variety of customised cars and bikes, and careful preparation needs to go into planning the route, equipping the vehicle, and deciding what to take.

Camping

Camping in Africa's mind-blowing landscapes gives flexibility that is hard to beat and it is tremendously exciting. Not knowing where you are going to sleep each night is all part of the adventure. Some of the greatest memories of an overlanding trip are evenings spent huddled around a blazing campfire, or falling asleep to the sounds of the African bush. In wilderness areas where there are roaming animals, you will never forget the first time you hear a hyena breathing next to your tent, or the sight of an elephant just happening to walk by. And nothing beats seeing the sun rise over endless dunes in the desert, or watching the stars from the balmy, tropical beach where

you're spending the night. Even those who have never pitched a tent will soon become experts at quickly putting it up and taking it down every day – even in the dark. Africa offers a range of surfaces on which to sleep – from gravel deserts and sun-baked earth, to springy green grass and luxuriously soft beach sand. How well you sleep simply depends on where you have chosen to pitch your tent for the night.

These days, thanks to the growing popularity of overlanding, campsites can now be found all over eastern and southern Africa. On the Kenya to Cape route it is possible to spend each night in a campsite, many of which are fully-equipped for overlanders. Most groups stop at the same campsites, making them great places to meet other travellers, as well as check the vehicle and get some rest.

National parks and game reserves have designated campsites, which must be used as directed by the park rangers. Some have extensive facilities, while others are very basic. But, after taking a look at how people live, Africa is not the place to complain if you aren't lucky enough to get a hot shower every night! The more established places have shared ablution blocks, taps, fire pits, rubbish bins, grassy or sandy camping sites, bars, restaurants and, sometimes, shops. Others have nothing more than a long-drop loo. Campsites in East Africa tend to be much more primitive than those in southern Africa. So bear in mind that, when travelling from north to south, facilities steadily get better, but when driving in the opposite direction, you will suddenly wonder where the swimming pool has gone!

The beauty of being completely self-sufficient is that overlanders can camp in the bush. Opportunities for bush camping vary from country to country. Some regions are too crowded to do this without attracting attention, while others are not considered safe because of the threat of robbery. Some, such as Zimbabwe, are largely fenced, whilst in other regions, such as Namibia, bush camping is illegal.

Pages 26–27
The ultimate overland vehicle not only gets you safely from A to B but is also home for a number of weeks or months, with its own kitchen, dining room, and bedroom.

This Spread
1–5 Camping out in Africa is an exciting experience, especially if there is wildlife within the vicinity of the campsite.

But, in many places you will find wonderful tracts of open space that make bush camping in the middle of nowhere such a special experience. For instance, in Botswana and Zambia, tracks lead off the main roads into remote wildernesses where game can be spotted outside the national park boundaries. Only experience will teach you how to choose a good site for pitching a tent, but avoid camping on what looks like a path through the bush, however indistinct it may be, as it could be a well-used game trail. Also beware of camping in dry riverbeds, as dangerous flash floods can arrive with little warning. When camping near water, stay a reasonable distance away from it – within walking distance, but far enough away to avoid wild animals arriving to drink.

Sleeping under the stars in Africa without a tent is a wonderful experience but, because of the prevalence of malaria, you will need a mosquito net. In most campsites there will be a tree or fence from which to hang your net, or you can simply suspend the mosquito net from your vehicle. There will be some campsites where it is necessary to sleep in a tent, especially those in national parks where animals roam freely. In these cases make sure you're completely inside the tent, as a protruding leg may seem like a tasty take-away to a hungry hyena. This is especially true at organised campsites, where the animals have become so accustomed to the presence of humans, that they have lost much of their inherent fear of people.

Camping in or near national parks brings the added excitement of sleeping amongst the animals, especially when you don't know how many unseen eyes are out there in the dark. Big game will not bother you if you are in a tent, provided that you do nothing to attract attention. Elephants will gently tiptoe through your guy ropes and hippos will munch on the grass around your tent, without even nudging your flimsy home. However, if you startle them by making a noise, they are far more likely to panic and step on your tent. Similarly, scavengers such as hyenas and jackals will quietly wander round,

smelling your evening meal in the air, without any intention of harming you. They will also investigate the campsite rubbish bins for leftovers and will think nothing of making off with the odd shoe or saucepan if these items are left outside.

Cooking

Never mind coming face to face with a lion, the most daunting experience for most overlanders is cooking while on the road, particularly when they have to prepare a meal for the other 20 passengers. But it's really not that difficult, and you'll soon discover culinary skills you never knew you had. After a couple of attempts, you'll be able to control the heat on an open fire as expertly as the gas oven at home, and discover that there's absolutely nothing that can't be cooked over the flames.

Campfires create a great atmosphere and keep you warm on a chilly evening, but deforestation is a major cause of concern in some parts of Africa, so always use wood as sparingly as the locals do. Consider buying firewood or charcoal in advance from people who sell it at the roadside. Paraffin or gas cookers are carried on most vehicles in the event that it is too wet to start a fire.

When it comes to food, it's best to do a 'bulk buy' before setting off. Include dry goods, tins, spices and sauces that are not always available in some parts of Africa, as well as a few meals that can be whipped up when no fresh produce is available. Otherwise, fruit, vegetables and meat can be bought along the way and venturing into the local markets, haggling in strange currencies, and estimating how many carrots you need, are all part of the fun. The crew will always be on hand to advise – they are more experienced at dealing with prices and currencies, and know the best places to shop.

On a truck, the passengers are put into teams and everyone takes turns cooking, shopping and washing up on a roster system. Creating a meal together is a great way to get to know your fellow travellers, but, in some towns and cities,

1 Healthy lunches are usually prepared on the roadside.
2 Trucks carry all the equipment needed for cooking, eating and washing up.

3 Almost anything can be cooked on a fire, even in the rain.
4 The truck kitchen is very sociable.
5 Cooking teams take it in turns to prepare meals.
6 Charcoal is usually bought at the side of the road in sacks.
7 People are generally surprised at how well they eat on an overland tour.

"It always rains on tents. Rain storms will travel thousands of miles, against prevailing winds for the opportunity to rain on a tent." – Dave Barry

there is always the option of sampling the game and local food at some fine restaurants. Lastly, Africans (and overlanders) love to drink beer, and you will find excellent locally brewed brands just about everywhere.

Red tape

As long as you have all the paperwork in order, crossing from one country to another in Africa does not present too many problems. On the route between Kenya and South Africa, in particular, border officials are used to seeing overland groups regularly.

However, some borders can be easier to cross than others. Great care needs to be taken not to offend the border guards, who know that they have the upper hand, but patience is usually rewarded by free passage. Be careful with what you carry, as some possessions may be offensive to some countries and thorough searching of vehicles is common.

All visitors to Africa must be in possession of a full passport that is valid for at least six months after the finish date of a trip. It should have plenty of empty pages, particularly if you are doing a longer trip, as you will collect plenty of visas and stamps. It is advisable to allow at least one blank page for each country you are visiting. Getting a new passport in Africa is extremely difficult, so always keep yours safe. You should also take photocopies of it with you and keep these separately.

Travellers of most nationalities need visas for some, if not all, of the countries. On the Kenya to Cape route, these can be obtained at the land borders for most nationalities and are paid for in cash in US dollars. Before you depart, check the visa requirements for your nationality for each country that you intend to visit.

It is also essential that you obtain travel insurance in your home country. Your policy should cover you for personal accident and medical costs, as well as loss, damage to, or theft of personal belongings. Ideally, the policy should include repatriation in the event of a medical emergency. You should carefully consider a policy that specifically covers adventure travel if you plan to do many of the activities on offer. Insurance policies do not make for interesting reading, but it's worth the effort to pay attention to these details, as what you may regard as 'hazardous' differs considerably from the definition used by insurance companies.

Travelling overland in Africa does not require you to look as you do at home, so leave behind your expensive jewellery and don't bring your best clothes – they will only get trashed.

Not only people need passports – all vehicles, whether they are commercial trucks or independent overlanders, need a Carnet de Passage. This is an essential document that serves as the vehicle's 'passport', allowing passage between one country and the next. While travelling you must have the document stamped on your entry to, and exit from, each country you visit. The Carnet allows an individual to take a vehicle into a country where custom duties may normally be payable on importation of a vehicle, even for a short stay. The document is issued by your own country's motoring organisation and is a bond that provides security against you selling your vehicle in a

"Security is mostly a superstition. It does not exist in nature. Life is either a daring adventure or nothing."
– Helen Keller

country without paying import duty. A deposit to the motoring organisation is paid, and in the event of an illegal sale, the deposit will be forfeited to the country where the vehicle was sold. The deposit is returned to the owner of the vehicle once the completed Carnet is produced to the issuing body at the end of your trip. In most countries, third-party insurance is a legal requirement. Generally, you buy this at the border when you enter. Some countries, such as Namibia and South Africa, include it in the price of fuel.

All trucks have safes on board for keeping money and passports secure when they are not needed. If you are in your own vehicle, rig up some sort of secure box that is bolted into the vehicle and cannot be removed. Take along photocopies of all your paperwork and keep these separately. Some travellers scan copies of their passport and other documents and send them to a personal e-mail address that can be accessed in Africa.

Health preparation

There are no serious health risks when travelling in Africa if you come well prepared. You will need to update your vaccination card and go on a course of malaria prophylactics. It is essential that you consult your doctor or travel clinic a few weeks before departing for advice on what vaccinations you need for the countries you are travelling through. At some border crossings you will be asked to produce your vaccination card, and in some countries officials particularly want to see proof of a yellow fever vaccination. If you are on a tour, always inform your crew of any allergies and medical conditions you may have, or if you are on any medication. They are also far more experienced in dealing with African diseases and will know where to take you if you fall ill. If you are feeling at all unwell within a few weeks of your return, it is advisable to see a doctor. The symptoms of many diseases, such as malaria, bilharzia, or hepatitis, can take weeks or even months to show, and can be detected by simple blood tests.

Except for the very southern parts of South Africa, all eastern and southern African countries carry the risk of malaria. Tropical Africa accounts for 90 percent of malaria cases, which kill up to one million Africans each year. The possibility of contracting malaria should therefore be taken very seriously and you should pay careful attention to protecting yourself when you're on the road. Use plenty of effective insect repellent and wear long sleeves and trousers in the evenings, when

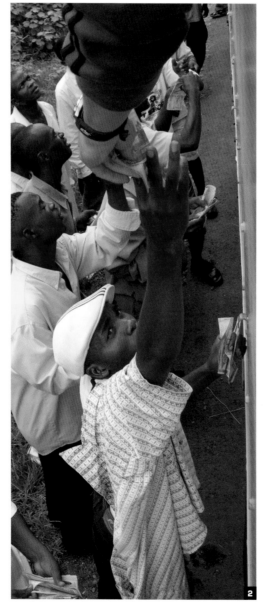

1 Help from the local people is often offered to overlanders at the side of the road.
2 Money changers can be found on most borders in Africa.
3 Crossing borders in Africa is usually hassle free.

mosquitoes are at their most active. Just because bites don't show on your skin doesn't mean you haven't been bitten. All tents have mosquito netting, so make sure that you keep the doors shut as soon as you put up your tent. Importantly, if you feel at all unwell, or experience any side effects from the malarial drugs whilst on your trip, tell your tour leader and seek medical assistance. All prophylactics are available in Africa and you may need to swap to another brand. Don't forget to take your drugs for the allotted time after you have left the malarial region.

Overland trucks carry a first aid kit for emergencies, but you may want to include a basic personal kit in your baggage. Independent overlanders should carry as much as they can for

Pages 34–35
Having a reliable 4x4 vehicle gives you the freedom to go off road and explore Africa at its wildest.

every eventuality, particularly if they are going well off the beaten track. Those going on longer trips should take a first aid course before setting off.

Photography

Photography is hugely rewarding on an overland trip. Not only can you take photos of the wildlife in the national parks, but you can simply poke your camera out of the side of the vehicle to shoot the changing African landscape as it rolls by. But, when taking photos of local people, always ask first.

Film and photo developing are widely available in southern Africa but not in East Africa, so bring plenty of film and spare camera batteries. If you do have to buy film on your journey, check the

"Tourists don't know where they've been, travellers don't know where they're going."
– Paul Theroux

expiry date. While there are a few places where you can get films developed in the cities, the quality is not always good and you may risk damaging the film. Rather wait until you get home. Sometimes conditions on the road can get very dusty so make sure your camera has an adequate bag. In fact, it is advisable to keep it in a plastic bag as well.

Other considerations include keeping your camera and film out of the heat, and protecting your equipment from bumps and vibrations in the vehicle. At some campsites there are power points to recharge batteries for video/digital cameras, and some of the overland trucks have power points.

This Spread
1 There is no better way of keeping a record of your trip than by taking photographs.
2 Overland trucks provide great vantage points for photography.
3 All types of other vehicles can be seen on Africa's roads.
4 Road conditions vary considerably throughout Africa.
5 Bush mechanics are surprisingly skilled and resourceful despite limited parts and tools.

"I travel not to go anywhere, but to go.
I travel for travel's sake. The great
affair is to move."
– Robert Louis Stevenson

Driving

Most of the roads used on the Kenya to Cape route described in this book are in good condition and you can complete the entire journey in a non-4x4 vehicle if you stick to the main roads. In recent years, there have been some major road-building projects and what were once decaying tracks riddled with potholes are now tarred super-highways. There are some exceptions and you will find a few stretches of bad roads, particularly in Uganda and Malawi.

Away from the main tar-sealed roads, there are a variety of road conditions to tackle, from sand and gravel, to dirt and clay. Some roads in East Africa are covered with a fine soil known as 'black cotton', which can become as slippery as glass and totally impassable when wet – you definitely need a 4x4 for this.

Unfortunately, road accidents in Africa are common, and caused by a variety of circumstances such as potholes, badly maintained vehicles, animals on the roads, and driving too fast on slippery or gravel surfaces. Road surfaces can vary enormously, so keep a constant look-out for potholes, ruts, or patches of soft sand which could put you into an unexpected slide. When passing other vehicles travelling in the opposite direction, always slow down to minimise both the damage that stone chippings will do to your windscreen, and the danger caused by driving through the other vehicle's dust cloud. If in any doubt about what lies ahead, always slow down.

Don't drive at night outside of towns unless you absolutely have to. Both wild and domestic animals frequently spend the night along the sides of busy roads, and will even sleep on the quieter ones. Tar roads are especially bad, as their surfaces absorb the sun's heat by day, and then radiate it at night – making the roads popular amongst passing animals. A high-speed collision with any animal, even a small one such as a goat, will not only kill the animal, but will cause severe damage to a vehicle. Kudu are attracted by headlights

"Stop worrying about the potholes in the road and celebrate the journey." – Fitzhugh Mullan

1 A smooth-graded unsealed road can become a quagmire after the rains.
2 Always beware of animals crossing the road.
3 A skeleton of a less fortunate animal on the side of the road.

which they may attempt to leap towards at the last moment. If you are driving at night, go very slowly, and be prepared to come to a complete stop if you see any animals on the side of the road. When you do drive at night, consider that you won't be able to assess the quality of the roads, so could fall victim to potholes and other obstacles.

In the game parks, the only animals that pose a major threat to vehicles are elephant and rhino – and then only those that are completely unfamiliar with seeing vehicles in their environment. Treat the animals with respect and don't irritate them by trying to move closer. Letting them approach you is much safer, as they will feel less threatened. If the animals are relaxed, you can afford to turn the engine off, sit quietly, and just watch as they pass you by. If you unexpectedly drive yourself into the middle of a herd of elephant, back off steadily and don't be intimidated by a mock charge – this is just their way of frightening you away. But, be careful not to drive or park in between a rhino and its calf. Once a mother loses sight of her calf – and rhinos have poor eyesight at the best of times – she may charge at the obstacle.

If you venture off the beaten track, make sure you have enough fuel and water. Navigation is also critical in remote areas. Carry a GPS, a good map, and a compass, and make sure you have the necessary recovery gear (hi-lift jack, spade and sand ladders). If possible, travel in convoy with another vehicle as, no matter how many spares you are carrying, or how much mechanical knowledge you have, you could suffer a terminal breakdown. In most places another car will probably come along sooner or later, but you should have enough supplies to make sure you are okay until help arrives.

Petrol and diesel are available in most towns and shortages are rare. However, for travel into the bush, you will need long-range fuel tanks, and/or a large stock of filled jerry cans. It is essential to plan your fuel requirements well in advance, and always to carry more than you expect to need. Remember that using the vehicle's 4x4 capability, especially in low ratio gears, will significantly increase your fuel consumption, as does the cool comfort of a vehicle's air-conditioning. In any settlement in Africa, you'll find informal mechanics and tyre menders at the roadside, and the continent's bush mechanics can effect the most amazing short-term repairs with remarkably basic tools and materials.

Finally, no vehicle can make up for an inexperienced driver – make sure that you are confident of your vehicle's capabilities before you take it into the wilds of Africa.

> "If you unexpectedly drive yourself into the middle of a herd of elephant, back off steadily and don't be intimidated by a mock charge – this is just their way of frightening you away."

4 Be prepared to get stuck in and get dirty if your vehicle needs an extra hand.
5 Overlanders should be prepared for all climates.

1&2 Before setting out on an overlanding trip with a motorbike, good riding skills are essential. As everyone knows, motorcycling is a dangerous pastime and no less so when travelling long distances over slippery and difficult surfaces. Although expert off-road riding skills are unnecessary as a prerequisite to overlanding trips, some experience off-road is invaluable. However, the real point is not the skills but the attitude – you need time and patience to undertake long bike trips.
3&4 Lunch breaks up a long driving day and allows you to stretch your legs.
5&6 After setting up camp at the end of the day there is time to relax.

Climate

Africa's seasons vary greatly and, on a trip between Kenya and the Cape, you are likely to travel through a variety of climates, encountering good and bad weather along the way. Although East Africa straddles the equator, many people are quite surprised at how cool Kenya and Uganda get. This is because, away from the coast, most of this region is high above sea level. Here, the rains arrive in October and November, and there is a pounding of rain on most afternoons before the sun comes out again. These short rainy periods are not too inconvenient whilst travelling, but you may want to avoid travelling in East Africa during the longer rainy period between February and March.

Summer below the equator is from November to February, when most days are clear, sunny and hot. Botswana and Namibia receive little rain but can get hot in summer and surprisingly cold in winter. These are desert regions where temperatures drop sharply at night and camping in the depths of winter (July and August), can be quite uncomfortable. South Africa, on the other hand, has a moderate climate all year round, although Cape Town is wet and windy in mid-winter, when Table Mountain is mostly under cloud.

The average day

On the road, the day usually starts with the cooking group rising early to make breakfast. Everyone helps with the clearing up, and then people are free to explore. When the truck is ready to move, the group breaks camp and loads up before getting underway. During the morning, the next cooking group will buy food en route for lunch, dinner and breakfast. The truck may stop to do some sightseeing, or simply head for a new location.

Generally, each day is different: some are long driving days, while others are non-driving days, when the group stays in the same place for a while. Once at the next night's campsite, the group unpacks the truck and sets up camp, and the cooking group prepares dinner. When in a town, the group often goes out for a meal at a local restaurant.

Cultural awareness

An overland vehicle passes through a range of landscapes and environments and there are plenty of options to meet the local people, join in activities and witness at first hand the daily lives of a diverse range of cultural groups. Remember though that you are the visitor and it is important to respect local customs, practices and religions.

For example, along the east African coast it is predominantly Muslim and it is inappropriate to wear revealing clothing, and in many customs it is impolite to greet someone without removing your hat. Never take photographs of people without asking permission, and always be friendly and polite. You will be well rewarded as Africa's people are very welcoming.

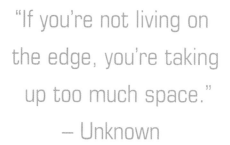

"If you're not living on the edge, you're taking up too much space."
– Unknown

KENYA

Kenya is a beautiful, welcoming country, and among the first words you will hear when you arrive is the Swahili greeting '*Jambo*' (Hello), and '*Hakuna matata*' (No problem). The people are friendly, the tourist trade is well organised and professional, and there's a lot to see, making Kenya a hugely rewarding place to explore. The country has a fine collection of reserves and parks, some devoted to marine life and natural beauty as well as game, and most activities are centred on the pursuit of the Big Five. 'Safari' means journey in Swahili, and wildlife safaris are big business in a country that boasts some of the most impressive natural habitats in Africa.

Kenya is situated on the equator and covers a 586 600-square-kilometre chunk of East Africa. The country boasts dramatically diverse geography and ever-changing scenery: rolling savannah where the Masai tend their herds, mountain forests full of indigenous birds, high moors of Kikuyu fields, and parched northern deserts. The roads, however, leave a lot to be desired. The tar roads are badly potholed, and all the minor dirt roads become quagmires when it rains.

Much of Kenya is situated in the Great Rift Valley, the vast, prehistoric fissure that stretches from Jordan to Mozambique. In the Central Highlands are the impressive Aberdare mountains, Mount Elgon, and Mount Kenya – Africa's second highest mountain at 5 199 metres. The Indian Ocean coastline features wide beaches and coral reefs in a pleasant climate, the medieval island of Lamu, and the mouth of Kenya's major river, the Tana Estuary. The tropical coastal belt gives way to an inland plateau of around 1 000 metres above sea level, home to 85 percent of Kenya's 30-million-strong population and the location of the capital, Nairobi. The semi-desert to the north covers three-fifths of the whole country. It is arid and empty, but offers visitors some beautifully stark scenery – this is Kenya at its wildest.

There are over 70 ethnic groups, and of the 40 languages, Swahili is the most widely spoken. Many tribes, such as the Samburu, Turkana and Masai, still live fiercely traditional lives and resist the advances of the modern world, and their striking dress and jewellery match their reputation as proud warriors. These nomadic tribes wandered East Africa for thousands of years before the peoples of the Orient and Arabia arrived on the coast between the eighth and eleventh centuries, mixing with the local population to create a new Swahili civilisation.

The Arabs remained in control until the end of the nineteenth century, when the 'Scramble for Africa' by European powers began in earnest, and the gin-and-tonic set came in search of pristine farming land and hunting trophies.

Kenya has two major cities: the high-altitude, colonial-era capital Nairobi, and the ancient Swahili

"This is a place for hiking, climbing, diving and cycling. Above all, it's a place for safaris."

Page 43
1 View over the Great Rift Valley which dominates much of Kenya.
2 Kenya is home to a diverse collection of African animals, including the Big Five.
3&4 Kenya's active urban daily life can be witnessed from the roadside.
5 A Masai warrior guards an overland truck.

Pages 44–45
Young Samburu warrior in northern Kenya.

trading port of Mombasa. Whilst these cities have an appealingly vibrant African feel to them, what really draws travellers to Kenya is the Great Outdoors. This is a place for hiking, climbing, diving and cycling. Above all, it's a place for safaris. The country has had to wage a war-like battle against poaching for decades, to protect its vast range of animals and birds in 50 national parks and reserves. Seven of these are marine parks – the rest cover a staggering 35 000 square kilometres of land. Here you can balloon over herds of wildebeest, or watch a pride of lions at work on a zebra carcass in the world-famous Masai Mara Game Reserve, point a camera at the many rhino in Lake Nakuru National Park, or replicate that famous photo of elephant standing majestically in front of Kilimanjaro in the Amboseli National Park.

KENYA'S HISTORY

Most of the 70 ethnic groups in Kenya arrived from other parts of Africa. Of the larger groups, the Turkana, Masai and Samburu settled in Kenya towards the end of the seventeenth century. They joined the existing Kikuyu people who are still the largest of Kenya's peoples.

The Portuguese, who arrived in 1498, were the first Europeans to settle here. They dominated control of the region until the sultans of Oman crossed the Indian Ocean and took control in 1729. Arabian settlements grew quickly at Mombasa and Malindi, and trade – mainly in slaves and ivory – flourished. Persian, Indian, Indonesian and Chinese traders followed, and the intermingling of Arabs and others with Africans led to the development of the Swahili (Arabic for 'coastal') culture and language. Swahili is now the mother tongue for the whole of East Africa.

In the 1800s, Kenya saw an influx of explorers and Christian missionaries, followed by European settlers. The Mombasa to Uganda railway line was constructed in the late 1800s, and Nairobi grew from a trading post and railway station into a large city. By 1895, the British had established a protec-torate called Kenya, after the 5 200-metre peak in the central highlands that the Kikuyu call '*Kere Nyaga*', meaning 'The Mountain of Whiteness.'

Kenya's status changed to that of a colony in 1920, when it was home to a large, prosperous British community, with most of the highlands owned by British farmers. Protests against the country's fertile land being allocated to the Europeans gained momentum, particularly amongst the Kikuyu, who wanted their land back.

The violent Mau-Mau rebellion, conducted by a secret society of mostly Kikuyu, initiated a campaign of terror on highland farms between 1952 and 1956. Many Europeans were killed or fled the country, but there were also thousands of African casualties: people were punished for supporting

This Spread
1–3 The Masai are a proud nomadic people and their imposing dress and jewellery are a testament to their rich culture. They are permitted to graze their cattle in Kenya's game reserves and the peripherals of the national parks, as traditionally this has been their grazing land for hundreds of years.

DENMARK

www.southing.com

Pages 48–49
The equator straddles Kenya and Uganda and crossing it is a milestone on any overland trip.

the colonial government. These on-going protests eventually led to Independence in 1963. Kenya remained part of the British Commonwealth, and much of the land reverted to Kenyan ownership.

Jomo Kenyatta became Kenya's first president, and served until his death in 1978. He was succeeded by Daniel Arap Moi, whose government was accused of corruption and human rights abuses. Despite this, Moi was re-elected five times before being beaten at the polls in 2002 by Mwai Kibaki, only the third president of the country.

For a time, Kenya was viewed as an African success story, but recent decades have brought difficult economic and political challenges.

The influx of refugees from Somalia, Sudan and Ethiopia has also placed a heavy burden on the government, but since the new administration began its term in 2002, the situation is improving and the outlook for the future is positive.

THE OVERLAND ROUTE

From Kenya's burgeoning capital, Nairobi, most overlanders head for the Great Rift Valley to the west of the city. This is the enormous cleft in the Earth's surface that stretches from the Red Sea to the Indian Ocean. Along the road between Nairobi and Nakuru, there are various viewpoints along the high escarpment overlooking the lake-studded African plains. The lakes of Elmeteita, Nakuru, Naivasha, Bogoria and Baringo are easily accessible and home to thousands of birds and pods of hippo.

Lake Nakuru National Park is the habitat of lion, leopard, warthog, giraffe and rhino. This shallow soda lake is particularly known for its flamingos, which gather here in their thousands, weaving a strikingly pink 'fringe' around the shore as they feed on the algae growing in the alkaline waters.

Most commercial tours continue from Nakuru through the western highlands, where tea – one of Kenya's biggest exports – is grown, and then through the town of Eldoret, entering Uganda at either Malaba or Busia. Independent overlanders also have the option of visiting lakes Bogoria and Baringo to see more flamingos, as well as the bubbling hot springs.

On the return trip from Uganda, most tours take in Kenya's premier game reserve, the Masai Mara, accessed from the Masai town of Narok. At least a couple of nights are needed here to explore the park. The Mara is crossed every year from July to October by large herds of wildebeest and zebra, as they migrate from the adjoining Serengeti National Park in Tanzania. Predators and scavengers

This Spread
1&2 Crossing the equator provides a perfect opportunity for a group photograph.
3 Northern Kenya is a remote region of hot gravel deserts and thorny bush.

follow in their wake, relying on the huge herds for food, and the sight is truly spectacular. From the Mara, the route goes back to Nairobi, before heading south across the border with Tanzania at Namanga. Other options for independent overlanders include visiting the coast, or other game parks such as Amboseli, Samburu or Buffalo Springs.

Nairobi

Nairobi is Kenya's capital and the city's Jomo Kenyatta Airport is the gateway airport to East Africa. It's a huge urban sprawl covering some 120 square kilometres with a population of just over three million. Nairobi steadily grew from a swampy workers' camp during the construction of the Kampala to Mombasa railway at the end of the nineteenth century, and by 1907 it had replaced Mombasa as Kenya's capital. Back then it was called *Ewaso Nai'beri*, a Masai expression meaning 'A Place of Cold Water', a reference to the chilly Nairobi River. The fertile farmland around Nairobi attracted some 80 000 European settlers between the 1920s and 1950s. Nairobi's famous Norfolk Hotel opened in 1904, and was once the social meeting place for this privileged community. Today you can still enjoy a gin and tonic in the colonial-style bar. During the twentieth century, the Kikuyu moved into Nairobi, considerably swelling the city's population. Today it's a modern commercial centre and the largest city between Cairo and Johannesburg.

Like many African cities, Nairobi has a vibrant, energetic atmosphere, with its bustling markets, alarming *matatu* (minibus taxi) drivers, potholed roads, dusty shanty towns and leafy suburbs. This is a place of contrasts, where it's not unusual to see a red-robed Masai tribesman pass a sharp-suited

"This is a place of contrasts, where it's not unusual to see a red-robed Masai tribesman pass a sharp-suited banker in the street."

4 Nairobi is the largest city between Cairo and Johannesburg.
5 Curio shop.
6 Nairobi National Park.
7 Daphne Sheldrick Elephant Orphanage.

banker in the street. Nairobi is also a great place to be if you want to get things done, with plenty of Internet cafés, post offices, lively curio markets and bookshops. Unfortunately, though, the city has acquired a reputation for being dangerous and petty crime is rife, so stick to the main streets and never walk around after dark.

Of the sights around town, the National Museum is worth a look for its extensive display of bones and fossils, many of which were unearthed by Kenya's famous archaeologist, Dr Louis Leakey. The museum's collection includes the complete fossil of an elephant, some tribal artefacts, ceramics and beads, as well as some of the 600 portraits of Kenya's peoples painted in the 1940s by Joy Adamson of *Born Free* fame (*see p61*). Across the road from the museum is a snake park, where you can see living examples of most of the snake species found in East Africa.

The Karen Blixen Museum – located in the old farmhouse where she lived from 1914 to 1931 – is on the outskirts of Nairobi. Blixen, who wrote under the pen name Isak Dinesen, famously began her memoir *Out of Africa* with the words: 'I had a farm in Africa ...'. The farmhouse was presented to the Kenyan government by Blixen's homeland of Denmark.

Slightly further afield, there are some interesting wildlife encounters on offer at the Giraffe Centre and the Daphne Sheldrick Elephant Orphanage, both a few kilometres away in Langata. The Giraffe Centre is home to both adult and baby Rothschild's giraffes, which visitors can feed from a tall walkway. The giraffes take pellets straight from your hands as you look directly into their faces, and it's a marvellous opportunity to get a rare, giraffe's-height view of life.

The Daphne Sheldrick Elephant Orphanage is a special sanctuary for orphaned baby elephants, which cares for them until they are old enough to be released into the wild. Visitors can watch them at feeding time, when their keepers give them a special formula in gigantic feeding bottles. A calf under two years old will die within 24 hours of becoming orphaned and left without milk. Young elephants need to be taught how to behave, and it takes endless patience from the orphanage's trained keepers to teach a baby to suckle, use their trunks and ears, roll in the dust, and bathe. When the calves reach two years old, they no longer need milk and are released into Tsavo National Park.

The Nairobi National Park is within the city's boundaries. It is so close to Kenya's capital city that it's possible to take a photo of a rhino browsing peacefully amongst the acacias with high-rise office buildings in the background. The park covers 117 square kilometres, was established in 1946 and is the oldest national park in the country. Animals include many plains game and the Big Five, except for elephant, for whom the park is too small. It was recently designated a rhino sanctuary and more than 50 rhino have been relocated here from remote parts of the country where poaching is rife. They have already begun to breed and will be used to restock other parks in East Africa. All in all, the Nairobi National Park is a very easy game park to visit, as it offers good roads and facilities. Half a day here is enough to spot a fair variety of animals.

If you want to experience game at even closer quarters, visit Nairobi's famous Carnivore restaurant, where you can sample a wide range of meats, such as impala and crocodile, cooked on Masai spears over hot coals.

Masai Mara Game Reserve

The Masai Mara is one of the best known and most popular reserves in the whole of Africa. At times, and in certain places, it can get a little overrun with tourist minibuses, but there is something so special about it, that it never fails to tempt seasoned travellers, documentary filmmakers and researchers back time and time again. Most of the 1985 movie *Out of Africa* (based on Karen Blixen's memoir) was filmed here. When Blixen crossed the Mara in an ox-wagon,

"…one million wildebeest…"

Page 52
The Giraffe Centre.

This Page
1 Guinea fowl.
2 Masai Mara Game Reserve.

1

2

1 View from hot-air balloon
floating over Masai Mara.
2 Young Masai warriors.

1–7 The Masai Mara Game Reserve is home to a diverse variety of animals and on safari you can often spot not only the Big Five (elephant, rhino, lion, leopard and buffalo) but the plains animals such as giraffe, wildebeest and antelope, scavengers such as hyena and jackal, and a variety of smaller mammals, reptiles and birds.

she said of the experience, 'The air of the African highlands went into my head like wine. I was all the time slightly drunk with it and the joy of these months was indescribable.'

The Mara is 275 kilometres west of Nairobi and covers 1 510 square kilometres of rolling plains, rocky outcrops and deep, winding rivers full of hippos and crocs. Although it's not the best bird-watching destination, its animal diversity is one of the greatest in Africa and all of the Big Five are easily spotted here.

The reserve is a natural extension of the Serengeti plains in Tanzania. There are no fences, and animals take no notice of borders drawn on paper: not only those that split Kenya from Tanzania, but also the limits of the protected area. The Mara River serves as the natural border and is the backbone of the Masai Mara. It is crossed every year by one million wildebeest and 200 000 zebras: from July to October these migratory herds move from the plains of the Serengeti, across the croc-filled river to new pastures in the Mara. The predators and scavengers: lions, leopards, cheetahs, hyenas and vultures, follow in their wake. Thanks to the constant supply of ready-made meals, the Mara has the largest population of well-fed lions in Kenya, and some of the biggest crocodiles too.

The Masai Mara was declared a reserve in 1961 to protect those animals that the 'great white hunters' had failed to destroy. The territory was originally Masai grazing ground and the local chiefs were made managers of the reserve.

The animals move outside the park into huge areas known as 'dispersal areas', and at any time there can be as much wildlife roaming outside the reserve as inside it. Since many Masai villages are located in the dispersal areas, over the years they have developed a synergistic relationship with the wildlife. Today the reserve is still owned and administered by the local Masai district councils and all camps within the reserve are run by the Masai.

The Masai people

The Masai are a largely nomadic, pastoral people who inhabit southern Kenya and northern Tanzania on semi-arid and arid lands along the Great Rift Valley. They occupy a total land area of 160 000 square kilometres, with a population of approximately half-a-million people.

The Masai have maintained a resistance to cultural change and still roam the plains with their cattle and sheep, living off the milk, blood, and meat of their livestock as they have done for thousands of years. Cattle are very important to them and '*Meishoo iyiook enkai inkishu o-nkera*' is a Masai prayer that means, 'May the Creator give us cattle and children'. The Masai believe that utilising land for crop farming is a crime against nature, and that once land has been cultivated, it is no longer suitable for grazing. According to their traditional land policies, no one should be denied access to natural resources such as water and land.

The Masai are characteristically tall and slender, and are most famous for their striking traditional dress of red, chequered blankets and intricate, beaded jewellery. They live in a polygamous family structure, where men have as many wives as they can afford, purchasing them with cattle. The Masai live in kraals – compounds made from branches and twigs, built to protect their livestock from predators – within which are mud houses.

Everyone has clearly delineated functions within the group. Women are responsible for making

8–11 The Masai are best known for their colourful and elaborate dress and beaded jewellery, especially their red robes and vibrant Masai blankets.

the houses, as well as supplying water, collecting firewood, milking cattle and cooking for the family. Warriors are in charge of the kraal's security, while boys are responsible for herding livestock. (Masai boys are circumcised in coming-of-age ceremonies and become warriors after spending an initiation period living in the bush.) The elders are directors and advisors of day-to-day activities.

The Masai have hunted lions for centuries, both as a test of manhood, and as a way of protecting their cattle from harm. The lions have learnt to recognise their red robes (and spears, no doubt) and instinctively keep their distance. They easily ignore all the vehicles full of curious people who get much closer to them, but one red-robed Masai far in the distance is enough to seize their attention and keep them alert to danger.

> "The Masai believe that utilising land for crop farming is a crime against nature."

Ballooning

There is nothing quite as magical as floating over herds of wildlife in the Masai Mara in a colourful hot-air balloon. It's a great way to observe the game and the savannah plains without the intrusion of vehicles and loads of other people all trying to do the same thing.

Flights start shortly after dawn, when the air is cool and calm, and the animals are at their most active. The inflation of the balloon is part of the show, and once it rises, passengers have the chance to watch the sun rise high above the plains. The flight is magically silent, save for the hiss of the burner, and the pilot steers the balloon over canopies of trees and woodland, dipping down to get closer to the game on the plains. After the landing, you'll enjoy a champagne breakfast under the arms of an acacia tree to celebrate your flight, and a flight certificate is issued on completion of the safari. Similar flights also operate in the Serengeti National Park in Tanzania.

Lake Nakuru National Park

Lake Nakuru is one of a string of shallow soda lakes that dot the floor of the Rift Valley, its algae-rich waters attracting thousands of flamingos and pelicans to its shores. The tiny 188-square-kilometre Lake Nakuru National Park is 156 kilometres northwest of Nairobi and was created in 1968 to protect the flocks of flamingos and other species in the hills and plains around the lake, including a very healthy population of black and white rhino. Nakuru was declared a sanctuary for the protection of these endangered animals in 1987, so you'll practically trip over rhino in the park.

It's also well populated with leopards, which are often spotted during daylight hours in the acacia forest at the entrance to the park – unusual for these normally nocturnal animals. You will also find several prides of lion, black-and-white colobus monkeys, hippos, antelope, buffalo and the rare Rothschild's giraffe. Game viewing is very easy and rewarding, and it takes only half a day to drive around the entire park.

The lake itself is in the centre of the park and is surrounded by huge white salt crusts, covering a surface area varying between five and 40 square kilometres. The number of flamingos present varies from a few hundred to several thousand, depending on the level of the water and their frequent migration between the other lakes in the Rift Valley. Nakuru's eastern and western shores are bounded by high ridges where there are beautiful picnic sites and lookout spots with fabulous names like Lion Hill, Baboon Cliff and Out of Africa.

1 Curio shop at the Masai Mara's airstrip.
2 Ballooning over the Masai Mara plains.

3 Flamingos.
4 Hippopotamus.
5 Warthog.
6 Rhinoceros.
7 Baboon.
8 Zebra.

The park lies only four kilometres from the town of Nakuru, the fourth largest town in Kenya and a thriving local centre with a bustling market. It's a great place to pick up provisions, buy curios and locally grown Kenyan coffee beans. Because of its proximity to the town, the park is fenced to stop the animals from sauntering into town, and at one time to prevent poachers from easily wandering into the protected area.

The town is so nearby, that it's not out of the ordinary to be able to watch a lion within the park, and at the same time observe a woman doing her washing outside her house beyond the boundary! A good advantage of the park's proximity to town is that the local people can get to know the wildlife – the park owns a bus which it regularly uses to bring in all the local school children for game drives.

The tracks are well maintained, though they get a little muddy in the rain, and the climate is good for watching game all year round.

Lake Naivasha

This is one of Kenya's most stunning Rift Valley freshwater lakes. It is surrounded by feathery papyrus, marshy lagoons and grassy shores. The lake itself is not a national park, as most of the surrounding land is privately owned, but there are several campsites along the shore from where you can spot the wildlife. Strong afternoon winds can cause the water to get very rough quite suddenly. The local Masai used to call the lake 'Nai'posha', meaning 'rough water', which the British later spelt incorrectly as 'Naivasha'.

The lake – home to many hippos – is about 13 kilometres across, but the water is shallow, with an average depth of five metres. Interestingly, Naivasha inexplicably dried up at the beginning of the twentieth century and the land was farmed for a while, until heavy rains a few years later caused the water to return.

The region was first settled in the 1930s by the infamous British 'Happy Valley' set who bought all

the neighbouring farmland, much of which is still owned by white Kenyans. Around this time, Lake Naivasha was also Kenya's international airport, and 'flying boats' from Europe used to land on the water. Even today, when the water level is low, it's possible to see the wooden posts that mapped out the runway. This is still extremely fertile agricultural land, particularly for vegetables, fruit and flowers. Thanks to Kenya's new international airport at Eldoret, European florists are selling flowers 24 hours after they have been cut in plantations next to Lake Naivasha.

Much of the lake is surrounded by forests of yellow-barked acacia trees, which attract birds and black-and-white colobus monkeys. Visitors can take a boat on the lake to view the hippos, pelicans and fish eagles at close quarters and also to reach Crescent Island – a protected reserve where you can walk amongst the zebra, antelope and giraffe that come to the water's edge to drink. There are no predators here, so this is one of the few places

in Kenya offering the opportunity to walk freely amongst the animals.

Among the other attractions is Elsamere, the former home of Joy and George Adamson. The house overlooking the lake has been transformed into a museum commemorating the story of the Adamsons' relationship with Elsa the lioness, which was immortalised in Joy's 1959 book *Born Free*, as well as the subsequent movie. The Adamsons rescued Elsa as a cub after her mother had been shot, raised her, taught her how to fend for herself, and successfully rehabilitated her into the wild. The Adamsons proved for the first time that it was possible to rehabilitate lions and in later years, George went on to raise and release another 20 into the wild.

The 68-square-kilometre Hell's Gate National Park also lies beside the lake. It was named for its pair of massive red-tinged cliffs and was proclaimed a park to protect the variety of vultures and eagles that breed in these cliffs. The park is home to a profusion of plains game and birdlife. Again, as there are no predators, walking is permitted, making it ideal for hiking, biking and rock climbing.

Lake Bogoria & Lake Baringo

Lake Bogoria is a shallow Rift Valley lake 50 kilometres north of Nakuru and 25 kilometres south of Lake Baringo. It lies in a spectacular setting beneath the sheer 600-metre-high cliffs of the Ngendelel escarpment. Like the other Kenyan soda lakes, it has no outlet and the intense evaporation has led to high levels of salt and minerals. As a result, the lake has no fish but is rich in blue-green algae, which flamingos love – many thousands of them carpet the lake in a swathe of bright pink.

Freshwater springs on the shore attract an abundance of other birds, including raptors such as fish- or tawny eagles, which prey on the flamingos. In total, over 135 species of birds have been recorded in the area. Bogoria is also one of

1 Dawn glow at Lake Naivasha.
2 Campsite beneath the yellow-barked acacia trees that line Lake Naivasha.
3 Elsamere, the former home of Joy and George Adamson, now a museum.
4 Lake Naivasha has a number of picturesque campsites but be wary of the hippo that come out of the water to feed at night.

1-3 Thermal geysers and flamingos at Lake Bogoria. The rich birdlife here is attracted by the high level of salt and minerals in the water.

the best places in Kenya to see greater kudu, as well as buffalo, zebra and impala.

The 32-square-kilometre lake is still volcanically active, and the western shore is lined with spouting geysers, spurting steam and bubbling geothermal pools. The thermal geysers can shoot spumes of hot spray up to six metres high and visitors are warned not to get too close. If you want to stay over here, the Fig Tree Campsite is a scenic spot where welcome shade is provided by the massive fig trees.

Further north, Lake Baringo is the most northerly of the Rift Valley lakes. Like Naivasha, the 130-square-kilometre lake is also freshwater, and it teems with crocodiles, hippos and an abundance of fish, which in turn attract pelicans, cormorants and fish eagles. Over 470 species of birds have been recorded at Baringo and it's one of Kenya's top destinations for bird-watching.

In the middle of the lake is Ol Kokwe, a stark, rocky island that's home to a village and well appointed camp – an excellent base for exploring the lake on boats in search of hippos and birds. The local Njemp people are not afraid of the resident crocodiles and they fish in the lake from their canoes. It is thought that the sheer numbers of fish keep the crocodiles satisfied, preventing them from going after any mammal meat.

Samburu, Buffalo Springs & Shaba game reserves

Just north of Isiolo, and around 325 kilometres north of Nairobi, are the Samburu, Buffalo Springs and Shaba game reserves – some of the most remote and least visited of Kenya's game parks. They are located in the country's hot and arid northern region – when you see a camel train walking single file along a dry riverbed, you know you're in a pretty parched area.

The three reserves cover around 300 square kilometres in total and are separated by the Ewaso Nyiro River, which provides water for the animals, including the local goats and sheep, and some relief from the equatorial sun. You'll find a narrow

1 Marabou stork.
2 Driving down the Rift Valley escarpment towards Lake Bogoria.
3 The northern regions of Kenya are drier and harsher than the south, but equally scenic.

stretch of palms and woodland along the river, and away from this is acacia woodland and hot, dusty scrubland. This desolate landscape is the preferred habitat for some mammals that have adapted well to the harsh environment. Among these are Grevy's zebra, reticulated giraffe and Beisa Oryx – species only found north of the equator and not in Kenya's other parks. Elephants, cheetahs, vervet monkeys, hippos and crocodiles inhabit the river. The long-necked gerenuk, also known as the giraffe-necked antelope, is an unusual animal that spends much of its time on its hind legs reaching up to eat the withered bushes.

Buffalo Springs is south of the river from Samburu and, unlike Samburu, has populations of the common zebra as well as the Grevy's zebra. It's an unexplained phenomenon why the common zebra is not found on the north side of the river.

Shaba, the largest of the three – and the most inaccessible (4x4 only) – has a doubtful place in the history of Kenya's game conservation. It was here that Joy Adamson was murdered in 1980 while she was attempting to introduce a rehabilitated leopard into the reserve.

The colourful Samburu people in this region live the same nomadic, pastoralist lifestyle as they have done for hundreds of years. Close relatives of the Masai in the south, they wear similar bright clothing and jewellery.

If you want to visit this region, think carefully about when to go, as daytime temperatures regularly reach 40 degrees Celsius between January and October, even when it rains.

Mount Kenya National Park

At 5 199 metres, Mount Kenya is the highest mountain in Kenya, and the second highest in Africa, after Kilimanjaro in neighbouring Tanzania. It is 175 kilometres north of Nairobi and 10 kilometres south of the equator, and despite this is crowned with gleaming, snow-covered peaks. It's a huge mountain, in circumference as well as height, with a diameter of around 120 kilometres. In Kikuyu, the mountain is known as '*Kere Nyaga*', meaning 'Mountain of Whiteness', and is the seat of the fabled god, Ghai. The Kikuyu, who live on the slopes, always build their homes facing this sacred peak.

Part of the mountain's magic is the variation in flora and fauna as the altitude changes. The lower slopes are covered with dry forest, but above 2 000 metres is true afro-montane forest of cedar and podo trees. At 2 500 metres, a dense belt of bamboo grows up to 12 metres high. Higher still, forests of giant heather grow and glades are covered with high-altitude moss. From 4 500 metres up to the snow line, there is open moorland where bizarre-looking giant lobelia grow. At the very top you will find permanent ice in some 11 glacier lakes. Due to global warming, however,

"One who never travels thinks it is only his mother who is a good cook." – Kikuyu proverb

4 A curious elephant.
5 Long-necked gerenuk.
6&7 Every year thousands of hikers undertake the climb to the top of Point Lenana on Mount Kenya.

these are shrinking fast and seven glaciers have already disappeared in the last 100 years.

Fewer people go trekking on Mount Kenya than Kilimanjaro, but those who do rate the experience far higher than the Kili climb (*see p115*). The easiest route – and one that's open to all trekkers – is to Point Lenana at 4 985 metres, commonly dubbed the Tourist Peak. The trek is an excellent opportunity to enjoy the beautiful scenery on the mountain and the snow on the equator. Only experienced climbers can climb the highest peaks of Nelion or Batian at 5 199 metres, as this involves the use of specialised climbing gear.

Amboseli National Park

Amboseli has been made famous by the photographs of elephants taken there, with snow-capped Kilimanjaro in the background. It's a small but well-established national park 240 kilometres southeast of Nairobi, on the border with Tanzania.

The name comes from the Masai word '*empusel*',

which means 'salty dust'. It arises from the time, some thousand years ago, when Kilimanjaro erupted and covered the area with volcanic ash. The landscape of open plains, trampled by hundreds of animals, still looks dry and dusty but the area is well-watered, thanks to the ice cap on the top of Kilimanjaro only 25 kilometres away in Tanzania. This constantly feeds two springs in the middle of the park. There are 900 elephants in the park, which reputedly have the biggest tusks in Kenya. There's also an abundance of plains game, and big cats include lion, leopard and cheetah.

Amboseli was gazetted a national park in 1974 in an attempt to stop rampant poaching and hunting – unfortunately, rhinos have been wiped out here. As with other East African parks, the Masai – the ancestral inhabitants of the land – were sent to live outside the new park's boundaries. Today they live peacefully on the edge of the park and are very protective of their local wildlife.

Amboseli is one of the most popular parks in

Page 66–67
Mount Kilimanjaro in Tanzania is only a few kilometres over Kenya's southern border.

This Page
1–4 Amboseli National Park offers good game viewing on the open plains, and on a clear day when the cloud lifts, there are dramatic views of snow-capped Mount Kilimanjaro.

Kenya, as it provides wonderful game viewing throughout the year. It has an excellent network of roads, the best of which are found around the central swamp areas and springs, and at the lookout on Observation Hill.

Mombasa

Mombasa is Kenya's second-largest city, with a population of around 600 000, and is East Africa's main port. It is built on a 15-square-kilometre island and linked to the mainland by a causeway and a rickety old ferry.

The city has a history dating back more than 2 000 years, when the Persians, Arabs, Indians and Chinese first visited the East African coast to trade in slaves, animal hides, ivory and spices. The British arrived in 1873 and built the Mombasa–Kampala railway and the Kilindini Harbour, and began to develop tourist facilities along the coast.

Today, there's a long line of top-class beachside hotels just south of the Old Town centred around Diani Beach, and a selection of backpackers' resorts and campsites on Tiwi Beach that are ideal for a budget break. Beaches are of fine white sand and there are plenty of activities on offer, including diving, snorkelling, windsurfing and jet-skiing.

"The landscape of open plains, trampled by hundreds of animals, still looks dry and dusty but the area is well-watered, thanks to the ice cap on the top of Kilimanjaro only 25 kilometres away in Tanzania."

There are several marine national parks off the Kenyan coast that can be visited by dhow or glass-bottomed boat. Established between 1968 and 1975, these were the first of their kind in Africa.

The long coral reef that stretches along Kenya's entire coastline has been protected from over-fishing by marine park laws and attracts a myriad of fish – over 250 species, as well as over 40 species of coral. The more unusual species of sea creature include 150-year-old giant clams and the rare dugong, a half-mammal, half-fish that appears to have 'breasts', causing early fishermen to believe in mermaids. There are some 800 turtles living along the coast, including a number of loggerhead and giant leatherback turtles.

In Mombasa itself, the narrow streets are crowded with Arab-inspired houses and their elaborately carved doorways. The city's most famous landmark is two pairs of concrete elephant tusks created as a ceremonial arch to commemorate the coronation of Queen Elizabeth II in 1953. Also worth a look is the crumbly Fort Jesus in the port, which was built by the Portuguese in 1593. It has wonderful views of the Old Town and houses an interesting museum with displays on Swahili life.

5 Mombasa port and old town.
6 Glass-bottomed boats visit the marine reserves along the coast.
7 Mombasa's famous tusks on Moi Avenue.

UGANDA

Uganda straddles the equator between the mighty rainforests of the Congo Basin and the vast savannah of East Africa. It's a place of shimmering lakes, lofty mountains and mysterious forests. Ugandans refer to their country as the 'Pearl of Africa' – a phrase originally coined by Winston Churchill – and it's easy to see why. For a small country no bigger than Great Britain, Uganda is home to some of Africa's major attractions. It is bordered by the fabled, snow-capped Rwenzori Mountains, a proclaimed World Heritage Site commonly dubbed the 'Mountains of the Moon' because of their eerie, glacier-tipped crags and giant vegetation. The country contains four of Africa's seven Great Lakes, one of which – Lake Victoria – is the second-largest body of fresh water in the world. The source of the Nile can be found at Jinja, where this mighty river begins its unstoppable journey north. And to top it all, the Pearl of Africa has the greatest variety of primates anywhere in Africa – including chimpanzees and the highly endangered mountain gorillas.

However, Uganda has had a turbulent history, and during the 1960s and 1970s it was regarded as a place of terror where the dictator Idi Amin shattered the economy and killed thousands of people who objected to his regime. It was during this time that Uganda lost many of its animals and the game parks were largely destroyed. In Murchison Falls National Park alone, 150 000 elephants were slaughtered by Amin's troops.

But Uganda has been politically stable since the late 1980s. Thanks to a democratically elected government and massive foreign investment, the infrastructure is back on track and this is once more a safe, easy country to travel through. Twenty national parks and reserves offer its wildlife greater protection, and animal numbers are steadily increasing.

The Ugandan people are some of the warmest and friendliest you will find anywhere in Africa. The population is estimated at around 25 million, divided into 52 different ethnic groups. When driving through Uganda's countryside, you will be bombarded by waving kids yelling, 'Hello teacher' – the first words of English they learn – and in the markets every trader wants to stop and chat. The overriding impression is of happy people who, surprisingly, hold no bitterness about their past, only bright hope for the future.

Uganda is a fabulous place to drive through overland, as this is the best way to appreciate all that the country has to offer. While there is a main, tar-sealed road that runs from east to west via Kampala, it is potholed in places and elsewhere are only dirt roads that get very slippery in the wet. But driving through Uganda's scenery is a delight – it is lush, moist, and incredibly green, with well-watered, fertile hills and valleys. Just about every known fruit and vegetable grows here. The hillsides and plantations are terraced 'Bali-style', and all over the countryside, subsistence farmers till their land and cart piles of green bananas, mangoes, and pineapples to market – a Ugandan market has got to be one of the most colourful places in Africa.

Seventeen percent of Uganda is covered by water – rivers, waterfalls, and the regally-named lakes of Victoria, Edward and Albert. The national parks and game reserves harbour ancient forests, craggy forbidding mountains, volcanic crater lakes and some very special animals. Without a doubt, the biggest attraction is the rare privilege of trekking into the forest to watch a family of mountain gorillas in one of their last natural habitats. Gorilla tracking is on offer in Bwindi National Park (a World Heritage Site near Kabale), on the slopes of the Virunga Volcanoes at Mgahinga National Park near Kisoro, as well as just over the border in Rwanda's Parc de Volcans and the Democratic Republic of Congo's Parc National des Virunga. The entire region is home to the last remaining 600 mountain gorillas (there's only one to every ten million people on earth) and this is the only place they are able to survive. An hour's audience is permitted with each habituated family and it often takes several hours to track them down. The experience is worth it though, as few other wildlife encounters can equal the feeling of looking a massive silverback directly in the eye.

Chimpanzees can be seen in Kibale Forest or Ngamba Island in Lake Victoria's Sese Islands, where there is a home for orphaned and rescued chimps.

Uganda's list of adventure activities is steadily growing. You'll find grade five white-water rafting on the Nile, challenging glacier climbs in the Rwenzori Mountains and even bungee jumping or quad-biking in the forests around Jinja.

"The national parks and game reserves harbour ancient forests, craggy forbidding mountains, volcanic crater lakes and some very special animals."

Page 70
1 People working on a tea plantation.
2 Most of the Ugandan people work on the fertile land, and Uganda produces a staggering variety of fresh produce.
3 Girl carrying giant papaya (paw-paw) to market.
4 Overlanders crossing the equator. The sign here is the perfect spot for group photographs.
5 Uganda has dramatic scenery of lush plantations and mountains.

This Spread

1&2 Travelling through Uganda's lush landscapes, it is hard to believe that this is a part of Africa. The hillsides are terraced in steep steps to catch the abundant rainfall and to take full advantage of the fertile soil.

3 Roadside markets.

4 Mountain road.

5 Rural village.

6 Marabou stork.

7 Uganda overland.

8 A curious little girl.

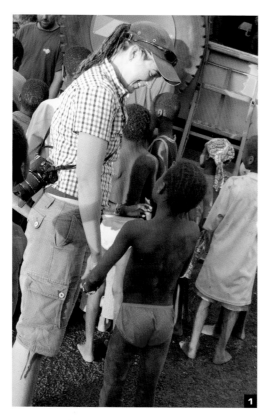

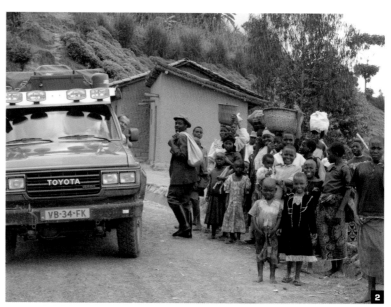

1 Local children.
2 Uganda's people are exceptionally friendly.
3 Terraced hillsides used for agriculture.
4&5 Camping in the shadow of the mountains.
6 Overcrowded local transport.
7 Ugandan children love to see visitors.

UGANDA'S HISTORY

At the time of the first European exploration of what we know as Uganda, three main kingdoms, thought to have their origins in the sixteenth century, existed – Buganda, Kitara, and Karagwe. The land before this time was probably occupied by bushmen and pygmies – the latter still live in remote forest regions of Uganda. Each of these kingdoms had separate laws and customs, and was ruled by a king.

The first Europeans to arrive were German missionaries in 1849, who sent reports back to Europe of 'great lakes and snowy mountains'. Then, in 1862, the explorer John Speke found the source of the Nile at Ripon Falls near present-day Jinja. The British colonialists were next to arrive and made Uganda their own in 1893 – hence the very English names of the country's lakes and national parks.

Uganda achieved independence from Britain in 1962, and for a brief time it was thought to have the best prospects for prosperity of any of the newly independent African states. In particular, the country's national parks had abundant game in lush mountain settings, and animal numbers were higher than in Kenya, Tanzania or South Africa. But it wasn't long – thanks to a series of inept and despotic regimes – before things started to go seriously wrong.

The first of the dictators was President Milton Obote, who banned opposition parties in 1969 and rewrote the constitution, putting all power in his own hands. Next was the infamous Idi Amin, who overthrew Obote in a 1971 coup and, in his inaugural speech, declared himself 'President of Uganda, King of Scotland, and Master of all the Beasts of the Earth and Fishes in the Sea'. A former sergeant in the British colonial army, the insane dictator directed a reign of terror for eight years, during which 300 000 opponents of his dictatorship were murdered and many more tortured. Ugandan society collapsed as he hit on the educated classes, dragging them out of their classrooms and offices to be shot for spreading the word of dissent to the people on the street.

Next to be targeted was the 70 000-strong Asian community, whose members were mostly traders and business people. In 1972 they were ordered out of the country with nothing but the clothes on their backs. Blatantly using them as a scapegoat for the troubled economy, Amin grabbed the millions of dollars and assets they were forced to leave behind. He then threw out the British companies

8 *Matoke* is a type of savoury cooking banana that is the staple diet for most Ugandans. The firm bananas are peeled like potatoes, boiled and mashed together, and are usually served with a meat stew.
9 Despite the hilly terrain, the bicycle is one of the major forms of transport in Uganda.

with interests in tea plantations and other industries, and once again squandered the millions of dollars in investments that they left behind.

Then, in 1978, Amin's insanity reached new heights when he invaded Tanzania. But he severely underestimated the force of the Tanzanian army, which joined forces with Ugandan nationalists and quickly counter-invaded. Amin was ousted and fled to Libya in 1979. Obote subsequently returned to office but soon found himself fighting guerrilla groups: the remnants of Amin's army and Yoweri Museveni's National Resistance Army (NRA). A civil war broke out, claiming another 100 000 lives. Conflict dragged on until 1986, when the NRA finally took control and Museveni was sworn in as president.

Peace and stability have returned to Uganda, the economy has grown, foreign investment has increased and many Asian Ugandans have returned to reclaim their businesses.

THE OVERLAND ROUTE

On the Kenya to Cape Town route, most overlanders enter and exit Uganda at the border with Kenya at Malaba or Busia. The first stop is likely to be Jinja, where there are several picturesque campsites on the grassy banks of the Nile, not far from where it tumbles out of Lake Victoria. Here, there is the option to go white-water rafting or quad-biking.

From Jinja, the main road leads to Uganda's capital Kampala, with its vibrant African street life of roadside traders, markets, and *matatu* (minibus taxi) stands. From here you can choose to go on an excursion to Ngamba Island in Lake Victoria to the south – the boat ride is half the fun and takes you over the equator. The 100-acre forest on the island is an important sanctuary for chimpanzees that have been rescued from circuses, and even from the cooking pot.

"When you see a man driving in a straight line along Kampala Road, he must be drunk"…local joke about the poor state of Uganda's roads.

From Kampala, you can either drive north to the Murchison Falls National Park, where the Nile squeezes through an impossibly small gap in the rock, or head to southwest Uganda, crossing the equator on the way.

It is the southwest that perhaps holds the country's greatest attraction. It's here that gorillas can be tracked in the rainforests of both Bwindi Impenetrable Forest and Mgahinga National Park, and where you go depends on the availability of permits. Both sites can be reached from the town of Kabale in the extreme southwest, which is surrounded by Uganda's lush, terraced hillsides.

Not far from Kabale is the spectacular Lake Bunyonyi, an irregularly shaped lake that Uganda shares with neighbouring Rwanda. There are a number of idyllic campsites on the lake's shores and this is a terrific place to wait for your pre-arranged date with the gorillas. Overland tours then retrace the road back to Kampala and Kenya.

Those with their own wheels can venture to lakes Edward and George in the Queen Elizabeth National Park – home to the densest concentration of hippos in Africa. The park is also home to thousands of bird species, and a highlight here is taking a boat cruise on the Kazinga Channel that links the two lakes.

Further north, along the border with the Democratic Republic of Congo (DRC), are the Rwenzori Mountains, which are all over 2 000 metres high. At 5 109 metres, Mount Margherita is Africa's third tallest mountain. Trekking and climbing here is challenging but rewarding, and there are outstanding views from the top into the rainforests of the DRC. At the foot of the mountains, near the town of Fort Portal, you have the opportunity to track wild chimpanzees in the Kibale Forest, and there are many rustic campsites on the shores of the picturesque crater lakes that litter the region.

Jinja

Jinja is the second biggest city in Uganda – although in population terms that's not saying much – and you are destined to pass through it if you are arriving in Uganda overland. It's a dusty market town that lies 80 kilometres east of Kampala and 143 kilometres from the Kenyan borders at Malaba and Busia.

1–3 Uganda's roads can become quite treacherous in the rainy season. The roads that wind through the hills are very narrow and accidents are common. When driving, exercise extreme caution.

Jinja lies on the banks of Lake Victoria and is best known as the location of the source of the Nile which, at 6 650 kilometres, is the longest river in the world. In 1862 the explorer John Speke claimed the Ripon Falls as the Nile's source but the Falls were submerged in 1954 when the Owen Falls Dam was opened, making Lake Victoria one of the world's largest reservoirs. The nearby hydro-electric station supplies Uganda and much of Kenya with electricity, and the main road between Kampala and Nairobi runs across the top of the dam. More recently, a second dam has been constructed below the Owen Falls Dam, and yet another is in the pipeline further upstream.

There's not much else in Jinja to keep you there, and most people soon move on to Bujugali Falls, eight kilometres upstream. This is a spectacular spot, with one kilometre of thundering rapids, forested islands in the Nile, and an abundance of bird life. There are also some lively campsites overlooking the rapids, and a number of adventure activities and community projects.

Bujugali Falls is the first rapid on a half- or full-day white-water trip through a turbulent series of rapids (*see below*). You could even bungee jump over the Nile on a jump that includes a water touch (*see p80*).

But, if getting wet is not your thing, spend time exploring the banks of the Nile, and the surrounding villages and countryside, by quad-bike (*see opposite*).

White-water rafting

The ancient Egyptians were certainly not into white-water rafting on the Nile, but at the source, inhabitants have been floating down the Bujugali Falls for centuries – in the old days, it was fishermen in wooden canoes; now it's thrill-seekers in bright orange inflatable paddle rafts, riverboards and streamlined kayaks.

Once the river spills out of Lake Victoria through the Owen Falls Dam, it soon quickens pace and hits

1

3

2

1–3 There are several rafting companies offering half day or full day, grade five, white-water rafting trips on the River Nile near Jinja. Trips start at Bujugali Falls, which is not the steepest of the rapids but the longest with about one kilometre of foaming water.
4–7 Quad-biking along the banks of the River Nile is a great way to meet the people in the local rural villages, and to experience the best views of the pounding water.

a 30-kilometre stretch of world-class white-water rapids. Most are graded four to five, so you're in for a turbulent time. Bujugali Falls is first up: a one-kilometre wall of raging water, followed by a series of 12 challenging water obstacles, including the legendary 'Overtime' – a 4.5-metre waterfall, and 'The Bad Place' – supposedly the largest commercial rafting eddy in the world. The idea here is to allow yourself to flip and be churned around, before your life jacket pulls you from the river's depths.

But it's not all about adrenalin – there's ample opportunity to drift in the calm pools between rapids, and stop for lunch on one of the islands.

Quad-biking

A quad-bike is a four-wheeled motorbike – an all-terrain 4x4 that can be driven by absolutely anyone who knows the difference between an accelerator and a brake.

The 'Roar of the Nile' quad-bike safari explores the banks of the Nile, and bikers spend a few hours travelling along trails that lead to a viewpoint from where they can watch the rafts bouncing on the river below. Riders can park up in one of the villages for a chat with the inhabitants, or buy something from a local store.

After the ride, there's time for a free-for-all on a purpose-built course, where you can practise your bike jumping or 4x4 skills, or get some tuition. For the more experienced, there are half-day, full-day and overnight safaris, for which a tent, lantern, food and drink are strapped to the front of the bike. This is definitely the best way to get right into the heart of rural Uganda.

Bungee jumping

Don't suppose Idi Amin ever imagined there would be a bungee jump in Uganda! But there is now one at Jinja, not far from the other adventure activities operated at Bujagali Falls. The Nile High Bungee, the brainchild of New Zealand's most experienced bungee consultants, is Uganda's newest attraction. Attached to a piece of industrial elastic, you take a leap over the source of the Nile to experience a few exhilarating seconds of plummeting through nothingness, feeling the space and silence like no other sensation in the world. A 12-metre-high steel

bungee tower sits atop a 32-metre-high cliff above the river. Jumpers can plunge into the swirling water 44 metres below – and we mean into the water, as a head touch is part of the deal.

Kampala

Kampala is situated 40 kilometres north of Lake Victoria and is spread haphazardly over seven hills. Its name comes from the Kigandan expression 'kasozi k'empala', meaning 'the hill of antelopes'. It's a young city that was only officially established in 1962, although a settlement has been here since Kampala was made headquarters of the Imperial British East Africa Company in 1890. With a population of around one million people, it's on the small side for a capital city.

Unfortunately, Kampala is a victim of 1960s concrete architecture. The office blocks and faded shopping malls bear testament to the addiction of European town planners to ugly, grey cement. After the civil war, when looting and destruction

destroyed much of the city, it remained cracked and crumbling for three decades. The buildings were riddled with bullet holes, and electric wires, sewers and drains lay exposed and broken.

But the city is now being fixed up and rejuvenated. The infrastructure has been restored and new hotels, sports stadiums and shopping malls are appearing on the skyline. It's also a fairly green place, with a number of attractive gardens, parks and golf courses.

The city centre is located on Nakasero Hill. The top half is where most of Kampala's parks are situated, with quiet avenues of large houses, embassies and international aid organisations. The bottom half of Nakasero Hill is a world away from this – it's a vibrant African myriad of shops, roadside traders, budget hotels, cheap restaurants, markets and *matatu* stands. The streets in this congested area overflow with people, battered old cars, and pavement vendors selling everything from rubber stamps to watches. The Nakasero fresh food market, just off the city's main drag, is one of the most colourful places in East Africa. Here you will find just about every fruit and vegetable you can think of, and some you can't – such as the ugly jackfruit or *matoke* (cooking banana).

The Uganda Museum has a collection of exhibits on Uganda's cultural heritage covering hunting, agriculture, archaeology, natural history and traditional musical instruments. The Kasubi Tombs, five kilometres from the city centre, are the traditional royal tombs of the kings of the Buganda Kingdom. Built in 1881, the collection of traditional reed and bark buildings is an important cultural site for the Buganda people of central and southern Uganda.

The Anglican Namirembe Cathedral is the largest cathedral in East Africa. The imposing building stands on Namirembe Hill, and some of the most prestigious weddings, including those of the Buganda kings, have taken place here. The congregation is traditionally called to prayer by the beating of drums.

1 Bungee jumping over the River Nile; you can choose to jump on your own or go 'tandem' with a friend.
2 Downtown Kampala is a busy place, but with a population of only around one million people, it is small for a capital city.
3 Kampala's hectic *matatu* stand; these minibuses are the most popular form of public transport in East Africa.

Ngamba Island

Ngamba Island, 23 kilometres off the shores of Entebbe – the lakeside town 50 kilometres south of Kampala – is part of the Sese Islands, a collection of 84 beautiful, untouched islands on Lake Victoria. This 100-acre forested island is Uganda's newest sanctuary for displaced chimpanzees.

Ngamba provides a safe haven for 40 to 50 orphans, as well as chimps rescued from zoos and circuses. They are now free to roam their island thanks to the concerned organisations that have raised funds for the project. For visitors, Ngamba offers a unique opportunity for close viewing of chimpanzees in their natural environment. Chimps in Uganda are routinely trapped and slaughtered for food, or captured and sold illegally as pets or circus performers. Once they have been captured, they become habituated to humans and it is sometimes impossible to return them to the wild, particularly youngsters who haven't been tutored by their mothers in the ways of the forest, and are therefore unable to cope on their own.

Ngamba Island offers them a playground of tangled vines and towering trees where they can live freely with no threat from the outside world. As chimpanzees don't like water, the island has a natural boundary. Visitors can view the chimps at feeding times from a raised walkway that provides excellent photographic opportunities. You can also watch them bound down from the trees for a rip-roaring tea party. Getting to Ngamba is by motorised Sese canoe from the pier at Entebbe on the mainland. The skipper will stop and offer you the opportunity to swim over the equator.

Kabale & Lake Bunyonyi

Kabale is a small rural town in southwestern Uganda, en route to sites for gorilla tracking at the Bwindi and Mgahinga national parks. Kabale and the nearby Lake Bunyonyi are popular overnight stops, and there's no shortage of accommodation

1 Chimpanzees were once plentiful in the forests of East and Central Africa, but today their habitat is threatened by deforestation and numbers have been reduced considerably. Conservation of the remaining populations is essential in order for the species to survive in the wild.

2–4 There are a number of rustic campsites on the lakeshore and islands.

5 The small town of Kabale is a centre of trade in the region.
6 Lake Bunyonyi is one of East Africa's most picturesque lakes.
7 The villages around Lake Bunyonyi are exceptionally friendly.

"Lake Bunyonyi and her islands are one of the most beautiful parts of Uganda."

in the area. Kabale is also where the Kampala road from the north joins the road to the borders with both Rwanda and the DRC.

Dusty streets lined with goods sheds, precariously overloaded haulage trucks, fuel stations and roadside mechanics lend Kabale a distinctive frontier-town feel. The region is heavily populated and extensively cultivated, and the town is the major trading centre for southwestern Uganda, making Kabale's fresh food market a must-see. The narrow passages are full of wooden stalls piled high with colourful fruit, vegetables, beans, grains and nuts, where traders bargain fiercely with their customers. The shops along the main road are consistently busy, with people from the farms coming in to exchange their produce for brightly striped mattresses, plasticware, second-hand clothes, blankets and water containers.

Lake Bunyonyi and her islands are indisputably one of the most beautiful parts of Uganda. Located in the hills six kilometres above Kabale, this picturesque lake shares its shores with Rwanda. The surrounding hillsides, as elsewhere in this region, are intensively cultivated in terraces.

Lake Bunyonyi is around 1 980 metres above sea level and is the deepest crater lake in the country – it started life a few million years ago as a volcano. It's also one of the few lakes in Uganda that is bilharzia-free. The surrounding forests, gardens, and farms attract a wide diversity of bird life, and over 200 species can be spotted here. Otters are frequently seen fishing in the lake, and night-time

brings with it a deafening chorus of frogs. This is a very scenic spot to relax, swim, and canoe.

Bwindi National Park

Bwindi National Park was formerly known as the Bwindi Impenetrable Forest. It is a magnificent green swathe of dense rainforest on the steep ridges of the Western Rift Valley in southwestern Uganda, very close to the border with the DRC.

This ancient rainforest succeeded in surviving the last Ice Age and is one of the most biologically diverse areas on earth. A recently proclaimed World Heritage Site, its unique and precious flora sustains roughly 600 mountain gorillas. Of these, there are three groups of habituated gorillas in Bwindi that can be visited on a gorilla trek – they are known as the 'M', 'HA' and 'HB' groups.

The Bwindi chimpanzee population is roughly estimated at 350 to 400. The nearby Virunga Volcanoes Conservation Area (Uganda's Mgahinga National Park, and straddling parts of Rwanda and the DRC) has a population of mountain gorillas, but no chimpanzees, making Bwindi the only forest in Africa in which these two apes live together.

Apart from gorillas and chimps, Bwindi is home to nine other primate species, including baboons and black-and-white-, red- and blue colobus monkeys, grey-cheeked mangabeys, as well as L'Hoest's monkeys. Bwindi covers 331 square kilometres of intensely thick and tangled

forest – hence the name 'impenetrable' – over a series of hills ranging in height from 1 000 to 2 000 metres. The flora is known for its exceptional bio-diversity. There are more than 320 species of trees, 10 of which occur nowhere else in Uganda, and over 100 species of ferns and vines. The rainforest receives some 2 000 millimetres of rain every year, so come prepared.

Apart from gorilla tracking, there are a number of other hikes and trails within the park, all accompanied by an experienced guide. It's a great way to learn about the other animals, birds, butterflies, trees and plants of the forest.

The campsite is in a stunning spot right beside the park headquarters. Facilities have improved

steadily over the last few years and there's now a lively village housing the park guides and trackers, as well as providing visitors with snacks and drinks.

Mgahinga National Park

Found in the extreme southwestern corner of Uganda 14 kilometres from Kisoro, the tiny 34-square-kilometre Mgahinga National Park is the country's smallest national park. It was gazetted in 1991 to protect the mountain gorillas of the Ugandan sector of the 434-square-kilometre Virunga Volcanoes Conservation Area.

Mgahinga is a dense tropical rainforest on the lower slopes of the volcanoes. The vegetation

2 The region around the Virunga Volcanoes is home to the world's only population of mountain gorillas.
3 Overland group photograph with local children.
4&5 The Virunga Volcanoes straddle the border between Uganda, Rwanda and the DRC.
6 Silverback gorilla.

includes bamboo, and lots of lichens and mosses – delicacies to a mountain gorilla. Only one group of mountain gorillas in Mgahinga – the Nyakagezi group – is habituated to humans and can be visited on a gorilla trek. The seasonal availability of bamboo shoots determines the movements of Mgahinga's gorillas across the Uganda-DRC border – they usually move to the DRC during the summer months (July to September). Despite the logistical problems sometimes caused by this natural behaviour, it cannot be controlled or predicted by park authorities, and tracking is suspended while the gorillas are away on their international holiday.

Gorilla tracking

The mountain gorilla is the rarest of all the apes, and was first 'discovered' in 1902 when a German officer named Oscar von Beringe shot two of them dead. His name, ironically, was attached to the subspecies *Gorilla gorilla beringei*. The mountainous region that straddles Uganda, Rwanda and the DRC is the only fragile environment in which they are able to survive. They have never been reared successfully in captivity and there are none in zoos.

These rare apes are sometimes not easy to find, which is what makes gorilla tracking such an exciting adventure. Permits must be purchased well in advance and the groups can be visited for one hour per day by six people (four for Bwindi's 'HB' group). The number of people is limited because gorillas are very prone to catching human illnesses – a gorilla can die from a common cold. Understandably, therefore, anyone who is ill will not be permitted to track.

Once you join a tracking group, the chances of sighting the gorillas are excellent, although it may take up to several hours to find them in the rainforest. Be prepared to hike through some rugged country: steep hills, thorny trees, tangled vines, and slippery floors laden with matted vegetation and mud all make the going difficult.

But gorillas have been located only 10 minutes away from the campsite before, and all groups are accompanied by an expert guide and trackers who follow the movement of the gorillas from the previous day. They make your path a little more bearable by hacking through the undergrowth with machetes.

Gorillas live in groups led by a male silverback – named for the silver band of fur around his torso that occurs naturally when a male becomes dominant. Gorillas are vegetarians and spend their days foraging for fruits, shoots, stems and flowers, all containing lots of water, so they don't need to drink very often. They communicate using a wide range of facial expressions, gestures and noises – just as humans do. At night, the silverback chooses a sleeping spot and each gorilla gathers vegetation to prepare their nest for the night. The trackers use the previous night's nest as a starting point for searching, and follow the flattened foliage and piles of dung that indicate in which direction the gorillas headed that morning. Finding them is hugely exciting, and your tracker will immediately motion for the group to stay quiet and drop to the floor. In those first few moments of hushed suspense, discovering that you are sitting only five metres away from a gorilla in the undergrowth is a spine-tingling experience. Your first glimpse might be of a baby in a tree, a female quietly munching on a branch, or even a silverback pounding his chest. Soon, more of the members of the group will come into sight as they – equally inquisitive about the human group – move closer and stare back. It's a great privilege to meet these amazing creatures in the wild.

Kibale National Park

Kibale National Park covers 766 square kilometres of pristine tropical forest, with some trees measuring over 50 metres high. The equatorial rainforest is best known for its healthy population of 500 chimpanzees. There are also 12 other primate species, and other mammals include buffalo, duiker, civet cat and the third largest population of elephant in Uganda. These forest elephants are smaller and hairier than their savannah counterparts. Birds are also abundant – there are at least 325 species – as are clouds of butterflies.

This enchanting park, filled with lakes, grasslands, marshes and forests, is 30 kilometres south of Fort Portal at the northeastern end of the Rwenzori Mountains in western Uganda. Fort Portal itself

"Sitting only five metres from a gorilla in the undergrowth is spine-tingling."

is nothing more than an overgrown village, but is a pleasant enough place to visit and is surrounded by tea plantations.

The highlight in the park is the chance to go chimpanzee tracking, as there are five groups of chimps that have been partially habituated to humans. Unlike the gorillas, they are less likely to be spotted, and are often found high up in the trees, or moving quickly away. On any such trek, you have around a 60 percent chance of seeing them.

Chimp tracking starts at the Kanyanchu Tourist Centre at the entrance to the park where you will meet the experienced guides and rangers – all with expert knowledge on Kibale's flora and fauna. Chimpanzee tracking lasts between two and four hours, and is restricted to four groups of four people

twice a day. If you are fortunate enough to find them, keeping up with them can be quite a challenge once they have decided to move away at high speed through the branches.

Murchison Falls National Park

Murchison Falls National Park is Uganda's largest national park, covering 3 840 square kilometres of hills, rainforest and savannah in the northwest of the country. The park is cut in half by the Nile as it flows towards Lake Albert, and it is here that the river has to squeeze itself through the famous Murchison Falls – said to be the most powerful natural flow of water anywhere on earth.

The Nile gains momentum above the falls thanks to the 23-kilometre Karuma Rapids, before

1 Chimpanzee in Kibale Forest.
2 Murchison Falls; view from the base.
3 Murchison Falls; view from the top.
4 Globe showing location of Murchison Falls National Park.
5–7 Murchison Falls National Park has a wide variety of wildlife that is attracted to the banks of the River Nile.

1

"The thunderous force of the water is so intense, that the rock actually shakes."

corkscrewing through an impossibly narrow seven-metre gap in a cleft of rock. The result is a powerful explosion of white water into the deservedly named 'Boiling Pot', 40 metres below. The thunderous force of the water is so intense, that the rock actually shakes. The Nile then widens and becomes placid again, its waters thronging with hippos, crocs, waterbuck and buffalo.

It's possible to walk from the top of Murchison Falls to the bottom, where you can experience the deafening roar and view the foaming waters. If you are up for it, there's a small eddy at the top where you can swim.

But, the best way to see the falls is from the river – a three-hour boat trip departs from park headquarters at Paraa and goes upstream to the foot of the falls, where you may catch a glimpse of a Nile perch being spat out by the falls. These huge fish (weighing between 50 and 100 kilograms) are strong enough to withstand the pressure of being forced through the plunging water. Some of Africa's largest crocodiles are found at the base of Murchison Falls. They grow to up to 4.5 metres in length, thanks to the ever-present Nile perch.

Queen Elizabeth National Park

The 2 000-square-kilometre Queen Elizabeth National Park to the southwest of Uganda straddles the equator in the western arm of East Africa's Rift Valley. It's bordered by the Rwenzori Mountains to the northwest and by Lake Edward to the southwest, and park headquarters at Mweya are 64 kilometres from the town of Kasese. The park wholly incorporates Lake George and is divided into two sectors, the north and south. It is split neatly in two by the Kazinga Channel – the body of water that joins Lake George to Lake Edward.

"Astonishingly, QEII has over a quarter of Africa's bird species and more than any other park in Africa."

The park was named, quite obviously, by England's Queen Elizabeth when she visited in 1954 and is still referred to today as the QEII.

The QEII once teemed with game, but that was before the civil war during which various armies looted the park of its wildlife – hunting for ivory, trophies, or simply massacring animals because they occupied the land being fought over. Since then, animal numbers have recovered, albeit slowly, and while the number of species is high, you won't find the quantities of game found in other East African parks. There are over 100 species of mammals and reptiles including some very old elephants (40 to 65 years old) that survived the massacres of the 1960s and 1970s; lions (some of which have been known to climb trees), buffaloes, Ugandan kobs, hyenas, leopards, monitor lizards, and a number of snakes, including pythons and cobras. The Kazinga Channel alone is said to contain the world's largest concentration of hippos, and a fair smattering of Nile crocodiles.

Astonishingly, QEII has 568 of Uganda's 1 017 species of birds – over a quarter of Africa's bird species and more than any other park in Africa.

The highlight of any visit has to be the boat trip on the Kazinga Channel, beginning at the park headquarters at Mweya. You can watch thousands of hippos at close range (this is where to get that must-have photo of a hippo yawning), buffalo and waterbuck come to the water to cool off – keeping a wary eye on the crocs – and the water's edge attracts thousands of birds.

Rwenzori Mountains National Park

To the extreme west of Uganda, 25 kilometres from the small town of Kasese on the border with the DRC, is the Rwenzori Mountains National Park. It's 120 kilometres long and 48 kilometres wide, and has been declared a World Heritage Site for its outstanding natural beauty.

The Rwenzoris are the fabled, glacier-topped 'Mountains of the Moon' that rise into almost permanent equatorial mists, their slopes covered

with gigantic, unusual vegetation. At the centre of the range are six peaks carrying permanent snow, three with glaciers. The beautiful, mist-shrouded, jagged crags, enclosing numerous lakes, create a 'Lord of the Rings' atmosphere, and are a distinct change in landscape from anywhere else in Uganda, or indeed East Africa.

The forests start above 3 000 metres and include giant forms of lobelia and heather. Indeed, all plant and tree species seem to grow unusually large.

The park offers superb trekking and climbing opportunities, with fabulous views and unusual scenery. The most popular trek is the seven-day circuit route, which can be attempted by novice trekkers, though you still need to have a high level of fitness. Treks start and finish from Kasese and at times the terrain is hard going, with vast bogs and slippery ascents to combat. You are accompanied by porters and guides and overnight in mountain huts.

1–9 The wildlife in Queen Elizabeth and Murchison Falls was greatly depleted during the 1970-80s thanks to Idi Amin's trigger-happy armies. But today animal populations are recovering slowly because of better protection of the parks.
10 Crater lake in Queen Elizabeth National Park.
11 Bananas (both savoury and sweet) are the staple diet in Uganda; each homestead grows their own patch of banana trees.

TANZANIA

Tanzania's natural environment and geographical features have made it one of the best tourist destinations in Africa. It's the largest of the East African countries, and almost a quarter of its landscape has been allocated to 13 game reserves and national parks, which are home to a staggering range of game. The Serengeti National Park and Ngorongoro Conservation Area have been granted World Heritage Status and, along with the Masai Mara in neighbouring Kenya, this important eco-system contains over three million large mammals. Many of these move around the plains of East Africa on a continuous annual migration – singularly the world's biggest natural movement of animals.

Page 95
A young Masai girl wearing
traditional robes and
beaded jewellery.

The main Tanzanian tourist activity is the safari – meaning 'journey' in Swahili – and the country's national parks offer the best opportunity for some first-class game viewing in pursuit of the Big Five. The town of Arusha is the safari capital of East Africa, and thousands of minibuses depart from here all year round to visit the vast plains of the Serengeti, the birthplace of man at Olduvai Gorge, the natural beauty of Lake Manyara, and the Ngorongoro Crater – which has the highest density of well-fed lion in all of Africa. It's worth bearing in mind that while the crater gets a little overcrowded with minibuses, the Serengeti is so wild, open and majestic, that travelling here is the true essence of the safari.

Tanzania's other, lesser-known, parks include Mikumi in the south, which is famous for its population of forest elephant. You will undoubtedly pass through it on any overland journey, as it straddles the country's main north–south highway.

In contrast to its flat plains, Tanzania has a couple of very tall mountains: Mount Meru and Mount Kilimanjaro – the latter is the third tallest mountain in the world. Every year, thousands of people fulfill their lifetime ambition of climbing to the top of Kili, and the experience is the pinnacle of outdoor adventure. It's rated as the most visited mountain in the world. It is also the only one you can literally walk up, rather than climb, but you need to go slowly to avoid developing altitude sickness, known locally as 'mountain disease'. Kili is famous for being Africa's highest point, at 5 895 metres, but a little-known fact is that Tanzania is also the location of Africa's lowest point – at 1 436 metres deep, Lake Tanganyika is the world's second-deepest lake.

With a long, tropical, coastal belt of white, sandy beaches and palm trees embracing the warm waters of the Indian Ocean, Tanzania is also *the* destination for beach lovers and watersports enthusiasts. The off-shore islands of Zanzibar, Pemba and Mafia offer the best opportunities for diving, snorkelling, fishing and sailing. It's even possible to swim with dolphins around the world-class coral reefs.

Zanzibar Island – also known as the Spice Island because of its long history of trading in commodities, from spices to slaves – is exotic, and steeped in history and Swahili culture. It's a place of noble Arabian architecture, romantic white-sailed dhows, and kilometres of palm-fringed beaches. A walk through the narrow, twisting

passageways of the capital, Stone Town, filled with beautiful Arabian architecture and elements of a fragile, Islamic way of life, will plunge you into the area's intriguing past.

Apart from many unique geological features, Tanzania is proud of its reputation as the 'cradle of mankind', as the oldest evidence of man's existence has been found here in the Olduvai Gorge.

Today, the country has a population of around 32 million, of which 80 percent is rural. When driving through the rolling savannah, you will frequently spot subsistence farmers tending the smallholdings where they grow crops of maize and pineapples.

"It's a scruffy old gorge, and the surrounding plain is flat and dismal… the place does have a familiar feeling. But it's the familiar feeling of disappointment when you go back to your home town. We come from here?" – PJ O'Rourke on the Olduvai Gorge

You'll also see people from the most well known of Tanzania's 120 ethnic groups, namely the proud, exceptionally tall, Masai herdsmen. They roam the plains inside and outside the national parks, which were their traditional grazing grounds long before conservationists earmarked the land for game reserves. By contrast, the Masai can also be spotted on the dusty streets of towns such as Arusha or Mto Wa Mbu, where the image of them riding on the backs of pickup trucks or buying cold drinks, brings their fiercely traditional way of life firmly into the twenty-first century.

Tanzania's capital city is Dodoma – a highly inaccessible city, thanks to the horrendous roads in the middle of the country. Although steps to move the capital here have stalled, the balmy port city of Dar es Salaam remains the country's principle city. Without a doubt, this is *the* place to get things done in Tanzania, and is the springboard for ferry trips to Zanzibar.

This Spread
1–3 One of the most evocative images of Tanzania is seeing the Masai wandering the plains.

TANZANIA'S HISTORY

Before independence, Tanzania used to be called Tanganyika. Its coast was the first region in Africa to attract international interest from the Persians, Arabs, Chinese and Indians who arrived in dhows between the eighth and eleventh centuries. By the end of the twelfth century, the mainland settlement of Kilwa was ruled by Persians until the Portuguese destroyed it in the early 1500s. They claimed control over the entire coast before being ousted, in turn, by the Omani Arabs in the seventeenth century.

European explorers and missionaries penetrated the interior of Tanganyika in the first half of the nineteenth century and two German missionaries had climbed to the top of Kilimanjaro by 1840. The eminent explorer David Livingstone established a mission at Ujiji on the shores of Lake Tanganyika. It was here that he was found by Henry Stanley, an American journalist who had been commissioned by the *New York Herald* to locate him, and who uttered those immortal words: 'Doctor Livingstone, I presume'. The European colonists arrived and Tanganyika was absorbed, along with neighbouring Rwanda and Burundi, into the colony of German East Africa.

Although the Germans brought cash crops, railways and roads to Tanganyika, European rule provoked African resistance. This resulted in the Maji Maji rebellion of 1905 to 1907, in which some 120 000 Africans starved to death or were killed by German troops.

When World War One broke out the British, who had control over neighbouring Kenya, Uganda

Pages 98–99
Overtaking Masai warriors on
bicycles with Mt Kilimanjaro
in the background.

and Zanzibar, attacked the German garrison at Tanga in 1914. The Germans won that battle but lost the war, and Tanganyika was awarded to the British. Resistance to British rule grew, however, and in 1954 Julius Nyerere, a schoolteacher who was then one of only two Tanganyikans who had been educated abroad at university level, organised a political party – the Tanganyika African National Union. Elections were held in 1960, Nyerere became president, and the British agreed to the establishment of internal self-government. Tanganyika was proclaimed an independent nation in 1961 and Zanzibar in 1963. The two countries combined and formed the modern state of Tanzania – a combination of both names.

Nyerere, who stayed in power until 1985, adopted a strict socialist policy based on that of communist China. Rural development was reorganised and farmers were moved from villages to co-operative farms. But the move was unpopular and failed dismally. It had dire consequences for the economy and had little positive impact on rural poverty.

Despite aid from China, the economy limped along without improvement, thanks to Nyerere's refusal to change his failed socialist polices in what had become one of Africa's poorest countries. To worsen matters financially, Uganda's despotic dictator Idi Amin decided to invade Tanzania in 1978. After several months of fighting, the unprepared and ill-equipped Tanzanian army did manage to defeat Uganda and pushed its troops back across the border. But the war had cost Tanzania 500 million US dollars and they received no international financial support at all.

Nyerere retired as president in 1985 and was replaced by Ali Hassan Mwinyi, who introduced market forces to kickstart the stagnant economy. The Rwandan genocide in the early 1990s had a major impact on Tanzania, as thousands of refugees crossed the borders. The subsequent war crimes tribunals were held in Arusha.

Benjamin Mkapa, who became president in 1995, has won elections since then and remains the country's president.

In 1998, Tanzania was the scene of one of that year's major international terrorist incidents, when a large truck bomb exploded outside the United States embassy in Dar es Salaam, killing ten people. Many hundreds more died when a second bomb went off at the same time in Nairobi.

Tanzania has been spared the internal strife that has blighted its neighbouring countries, but it remains one of the poorest countries in the world and is heavily reliant on foreign aid – despite this assistance, many of its people live below the World Bank's poverty line.

THE OVERLAND ROUTE

Most overlanders cross Tanzania en route between Kenya and Malawi or Zambia. There is one main tar-sealed road in excellent condition that runs diagonally across Tanzania and is effectively an extension of the Great North Road that crosses Zambia. Another road leads off this to the coast and Dar es Salaam. There has been some considerable road-building in Tanzania in recent years, and all the major arteries are in good condition.

As you drive into Tanzania from Kenya, the Namanga border is roughly halfway between Nairobi and the town of Arusha and makes an easy day's drive from the Kenyan capital. Excursions depart from Arusha to Tanzania's great game reserves to the west of the town. Commercial truck companies usually park up for a few days at one of Arusha's campsites, allowing passengers to take a multi-day tour of the Serengeti and Ngorongoro Crater by smaller Land Rover or Land Cruiser, which are more suitable for the rough tracks in the parks.

With the exception of the Ngorongoro Crater, independent overlanders can take their own vehicles into Tanzania's parks and also have the option of visiting Lake Manyara National Park. When visiting the crater, it is possible to leave

This Spread
1 Masai in their distinctive red blankets
2 A Masai kraal.
3&4 Palm trees on Dar es Salaam's beaches.
5 Truck manoeuvring through pool of water.

Pages 102–103
Ngorongoro Highlands
at the top of the
Ngorongoro Crater.

vehicles in the campsite at the top of the crater and jump on a tour with a local guide and vehicle.

Back in Arusha, the road heads south past the foot of Mount Kilimanjaro, and if the weather is clear, you may get a view of the magnificent snow-capped mountain – Africa's highest peak at 5 895 metres. Further south is the port city of Dar es Salaam, Tanzania's hub of commerce and industry and a hot, humid, bustling city. There are campsites on balmy beaches just outside the city centre, where vehicles can be parked for a few days whilst you visit Zanzibar, 35 kilometres off the coast. The exotic island is home to idyllic beaches, winding, cobbled alleyways, and lush tropical forests. Zanzibar has an intriguing past, as it was once a trading centre for spices and slaves, and a base for nineteenth-century explorers. On the northern and eastern beaches you can enjoy the Indian Ocean at its best: try snorkelling and diving, eat sumptuous seafood, or simply relax in a hammock underneath a coconut tree.

Back on the mainland, the main road heads southwest from Dar es Salaam and travels through rural Tanzania to Malawi and Zambia. This road passes through the town of Morogoro in the shadow of the Uluguru Mountains. There is a fantastic market here, where most overlanders stop to pick up fresh provisions for Malawi.

Southern Tanzania is largely rural and the road passes through scenic sisal and pine plantations, and small settlements belonging to subsistence farmers. South of Morogoro, 50 kilometres of the road passes through the Mikumi National Park, known for its many lion and forest elephant that can frequently be spotted from the main road. The road continues south via Mbeya, beyond which are border crossings with Zambia and Malawi.

Arusha

Arusha – 485 kilometres northwest of Dar es Salaam and only 300 kilometres south of Nairobi – is the major town in northeastern Tanzania and the halfway point between Cape Town and Cairo. Located at the foot of Mount Meru, Arusha is also within sight of Kilimanjaro, though both mountains are frequently hidden by cloud, especially late in the day.

The town was established in 1900 by the Germans as a garrison. Its prominence has increased in recent years, since becoming the headquarters of the East African Community and being the host town for the Rwandan war crimes

This Spread
1 Mt Meru.
2 Arusha.
3 Camel riding at Meserani Snake Park.
4 Game viewing on safari from Arusha.

tribunals. The International Conference Centre here has witnessed the signing of some of the most important peace treaties and international agreements in modern African history.

But Arusha is best known as the safari capital of East Africa. There are a number of national parks and game reserves within striking distance, including the Serengeti, the Ngorongoro Crater, Lake Manyara and Mount Kilimanjaro, and all overlanders will find themselves here on their way to these parks.

Arusha is a great place to stroll around for a few hours. The curio markets crammed between the clocktower and India Road are brimming with carvings, masks, beads and some unusual Masai crafts, and the fruit and vegetable market is worth a visit for its colourful displays. Shoemakers and tailors run their treadle machines outdoors, and women in bright sarongs carry bag loads of shopping on their heads.

Twenty kilometres outside Arusha, the Meserani Snake Park is a mandatory stop. There's a great campsite and lively bar here and, as the name suggests, there's also an excellent collection of snakes and other reptiles – the owners are experts on snakes in East Africa.

Serengeti National Park

The Serengeti, Tanzania's largest national park, supports the greatest concentration of plains game in Africa. Frequently dubbed the eighth wonder of the world, it was granted the status of a World Heritage Site in 1978 and declared an International Biosphere Reserve in 1981 for its natural splendour.

The name comes from the Masai word 'Siringitu', meaning 'the place where the land moves on forever'. These plains were formed between three and four million years ago, when ash blown from the Kilimanjaro and Ngorongoro volcanoes covered the rolling landscape.

The park covers a whopping 14 763 square kilometres and is the centre of the Serengeti Ecosystem – the combined Serengeti, Ngorongoro Conservation Area, Kenya's Masai Mara, and four smaller game reserves. Within this region live an estimated three million large animals. The system

> "The Serengeti supports the greatest concentration of plains game in Africa."

protects the largest single movement of wildlife on Earth – the annual wildebeest migration (*see Kenya, p56, for more details*).

The Serengeti's landscape ranges from the vast, short- and long-grass plains in the south, to the acacia savannah in the middle, and wooded grassland concentrated around the Grumeti and Mara rivers. The Seronera Valley in the middle is where most campsites are located. The Seronera Lodge is probably the most reliable game-viewing location. Here, it's possible to spot many of the Serengeti's resident wildlife, including giraffe, buffalo, antelope, hippo, crocodile, warthog and abundant birds. Large prides of lion can be seen moving stealthily through the long grass or even wandering through the unfenced campsites. (Look out for the Serengeti's adult males, which have characteristic black manes.) Hearing a hyena snuffling loudly at your tent pegs at night is a common experience.

During the wet season in February and March, one of wildlife's most amazing spectacles occurs. In only three to four weeks, 90 percent of the female wildebeest give birth, flooding the plains with thousands of newborn calves each day. These youngsters are easy pickings for scavengers and cats – very good reason why they need to be up and running within four minutes of birth.

The wildebeest may remain in the Serengeti for several months until the plains dry out. But, as these vast herds consume a staggering 4 000 tons of grass each day, they're eventually forced to march north to the fresher pastures in the Masai Mara.

The annual migration of more than 1.5 million wildebeest, as well as hundreds of thousands of zebras and gazelles, is triggered by the rains. The precise timing of the migration changes annually and is a spontaneous natural event. After the calving season in February and March, the wildebeest begin heading towards the western Serengeti in June. If you are in the Masai Mara, you can expect the wildebeest to make their arrival as early as July,

but they generally arrive between August and September and remain in the Mara between October and November. From December to January, the wildebeest gradually begin their migration back towards the Serengeti.

En route, the animals have no choice but to cross the Mara River, where massive Nile crocodiles with thickset jaws lick their lips in anticipation of a substantial feed. For any visitor, the herds are a spectacular sight: massed in huge numbers, with the weak and crippled at the tail end of the procession, and the vigilant predators hot on their heels.

Ngorongoro Crater

Tanzania's Ngorongoro Crater, another World Heritage Site, is a natural amphitheatre created about 2.5 million years ago when the cone of a volcano collapsed into itself. It's thought that the original volcano was higher than Kilimanjaro and internally combusted due to inactivity.

What survived is a 259-square-kilometre crater, which is 22.5 kilometres across at its widest point, and surrounded by a 600-metre circular rim. This is the largest intact caldera in the world, containing everything necessary for the approximately 30 000 animals that inhabit the crater floor to exist and thrive. About half of these are zebra and wildebeest. Unlike those in the neighbouring Serengeti, these populations do not need to migrate, thanks to the permanent supply of water and grass through both the wet and the dry seasons.

Pages 106–107
Game driving in the Serengeti National Park.

"The Ngorongoro Crater is a land of fable, and magical things happen there."

This Spread
1 Giraffe.
2 Vervet monkeys.
3 Leopard.
4 Lion.
5 Buffalo.
6 Giraffe.
7 Zebra.
8 Lion.
9 Hippo.

Pages 110–111
The Ngorongoro Crater, a World Heritage Site; the view from the crater rim.

"It's not unusual for a pride of lion to amble over and flop down in the shade of a minibus."

Visitors on safari are almost guaranteed to get a good look at some – if not all – of the Big Five. The King of the Beasts lords it over the crater, which reputedly supports the densest population of lion in Africa. There are also leopard, cheetah, hyena, large herds of buffalo, and Tanzania's few remaining black rhino. The crater's elephants are mostly old bulls with giant tusks. The females and calves prefer the forested highlands on the crater rim and rarely venture down into the grasslands. There are no giraffe here – they can't climb down the crater's steep sides, and there is also a lack of food to munch on at tree level.

The crater floor consists mainly of grassy plains broken by a few tracts of woodland. The main water source is Lake Migadi in the centre of the crater – a soda lake that attracts flocks of pink-winged flamingos and plenty of contented hippos. The views from the rim overlooking Ngorongoro Crater are sensational, and you can pick out the wildlife as dots on the crater floor. Safaris descend the steep road into the crater just after dawn. Thanks to the army of minibuses that go down each day, the animals are not afraid of Toyota Land Cruisers or the camera-touting tourists – it's not unusual for a pride of lion to amble over and flop down in the shade provided by a stationary minibus.

There is a campsite at the top of the crater but, as the top is 600 metres above the crater floor, it gets very chilly here at night. The Ngorongoro Crater is not a national park but rather a conservation area, declared as such to protect the local Masai's grazing rights (they'd already lost grazing land when the Serengeti was annexed as a park in 1951). Even today in the crater, despite the heavy presence of lion, you'll see the occasional red-robed Masai herdsman tending his rather nervous-looking cows.

Olduvai Gorge

On the vast plains between the rim of the Ngorongoro Crater and the Serengeti's Naabi Hill gate lies the Olduvai Gorge, a crack in the flat earth also referred to as the 'cradle of mankind'.

Veer off the main road that carries the army of safari minibuses between the two game reserves, to visit the tiny Olduvai Gorge Museum perched on the lip of the spectacular valley. Exhibits document the archaeological significance of the area since the first excavations in 1911, when a German professor looking for butterflies accidentally came across prehistoric fossilised bones.

Louis Leakey and his wife, Mary, first began digging in 1933, and a quarter of a century later they found the fragmented skull of the 'Nutcracker Man', dating back to 1.75 million BC. A year later, another skull and set of bones was unearthed – a small, hunched, ape-like creature with a large brain, which lived in Tanzania some two million years ago. Nicknamed 'Handyman' because of stone tools found nearby, this is believed to be modern man's direct ancestor.

Then, in 1979 the Leakeys made another discovery that further pushed back the date of the emergence of mankind: fossilised footprints of upright two-legged creatures – a man, woman and child – over 3.5 million years old.

A total of 35 human remains have been discovered in the gorge, as well as those of prehistoric animals – the Deinotheruium, an elephant-like creature with downward-curving tusks, and the Hipparion, a three-toed horse.

Lake Manyara National Park

About 130 kilometres from Arusha near the small town of Mto Wa Mbu, this park is often overlooked in favour of the other two giants, which is a pity as it offers some unusual and scenic game viewing.

"Masai warriors tend the tiny, two-roomed museum."

This Spread
1 Looking down on to the Ngorongoro Crater floor.
2 Black-maned male lions.
3 The crater's large bull elephants.
4 Elephant in acacia forest.
5 Hippo.
6 Hyena on the edge of Lake Migadi.
7 Olduvai Gorge.

The word Manyara is derived from 'emanyara', a Masai name for a type of sturdy plant that they traditionally grow to make cattle stockades – you'll find a specimen of it at Manyara's entrance gate.

The park covers 325 square kilometres and is relatively small, owing to the fact that two thirds is covered by the alkaline Lake Manyara. The remaining third is a slice of marshes, grassland and acacia woodland tucked between the lake itself and the Rift Valley escarpment, whose red-brown wall looms 600 metres on the eastern horizon. There are fabulous views over Manyara from the road that climbs up this escarpment from Mto Wa Mbu towards the crater.

"At the top, exhaustion fades away..."

Manyara's plains game include buffalo, wildebeest, giraffe and hyena, and pods of hippo can be found in the Simba River. Pelicans, storks, geese, herons and cormorants share Lake Manyara with migrant flamingos, which turn the crystalline edges of the soda lake a vibrant pink. Manyara is also renowned as the home of the famous tree-climbing lions. The park is

1–2 Lake Manyara National Park has sizeable populations of elephant and hippo.

also the ideal location for elephant because of its abundance of tree- and plant-life – Manyara has Tanzania's highest population of elephant per square kilometre.

Mount Kilimanjaro

Tanzania's snow-capped Mount Kilimanjaro, affectionately known as Kili, is the tallest mountain in Africa and the third highest in the world. Kili isn't part of a high mountain range but rises in complete isolation – its towering cone a world-recognised image of Africa. At 5 895 metres, it's also the highest free-standing mountain on Earth and comprises one extinct volcano – Shira, at 3 962 metres, and two dormant volcanoes, Mawenzi at 5 149 metres, and Kibo at 5 895 metres. Kibo was still active 360 000 years ago but all three peaks have been pretty well-behaved since then.

A World Heritage Site since 1989, the Kilimanjaro National Park covers an area of approximately 755 square kilometres. It's about 120 kilometres from Arusha – though the nearest large town is

Moshi – and the road between Arusha and Dar es Salaam goes past its southern base. The mountain has its own micro-climate and the rain-shadow to the south and east supplies Arusha and Moshi with fertile land full of banana groves and coffee plantations. It's assumed that the mountain got its name from the Swahili word '*Kilima*', meaning 'Top of the Hill'.

Climbing Kilimanjaro is the adventure of a lifetime for many visitors to Tanzania, and about 20 000 people climb it every year. It's the highest 'walkable' mountain in the world, can be climbed without ropes or technical expertise, and is rated as the most visited mountain on the planet. Despite this, hiking up is physically and mentally demanding. Because of altitude sickness, as many as 40 percent of those who attempt the climb don't make it to the top. This can set in at above 3 000 metres, when climbers experience loss of appetite, nausea and headaches. There's no prior indication as to who might suffer from altitude sickness (fitness, age and experience are irrelevant), and the only cure is an immediate descent to a lower altitude.

There are several routes and organised treks up the mountain. These usually last between five and eight days, and are graded according to level of difficulty – though porters carry your gear. The last slog up the mountain is hard and you make the final ascent just after midnight in subzero temperatures to reach Uhuru Peak in time for the sunrise. At the top, exhaustion fades away as the sun ascends above the 'Roof of Africa'.

The mountain supports a unique combination of climatic zones that take you on the equivalent of a trip from the equator to the Arctic in just over a few days. The cultivated lower slopes lead into rich rainforest inhabited by leopard, elephant, antelope and buffalo. Above the forest is moorland dotted with giant lobelias and massive heathers. The barren and cold Alpine desert is just below the snow line. From 4 000 to 5 000 metres, the temperature of this desert zone ranges from subzero at night to 30 degrees Celsius during the day. There are permanent glaciers at the top. The ice cap on Kibo peak is over two kilometres wide but, as with Mount Kenya, Kili's glaciers have started to erode because of global warming. The ice is receding at such a rate that there is concern it may disappear completely within the next 20 years. Thirty-three percent of Kilimanjaro's ice has disappeared in the last two decades – 82 percent since 1912.

3–6 When the cloud lifts, the snow-capped peaks of Mt Kilimanjaro can be seen from quite a distance. Every year an estimated 20 000 people attempt the climb to the top.

Dar es Salaam

Dar es Salaam, Tanzania's largest city and one of East Africa's most important ports, is affectionately referred to as simply 'Dar'. In 1973, Dodoma in the middle of the country was somewhat absurdly appointed the new capital of Tanzania, but most government functions remain in Dar, and it's still the country's premier city.

Dar es Salaam is an Arabic term meaning 'Haven of Peace', though it's hardly peaceful but rather a hustling, bustling, humid port that you will pass through en route to Zanzibar, only 35 kilometres off the coast. Frequent ferries and hydrofoils link Dar es Salaam with Zanzibar and the neighbouring islands of Pemba and Mafia. The city's many campsites have facilities for overlanders to park their vehicles securely for a few days while visiting Zanzibar.

Dar was founded in 1866 by the Sultan of Zanzibar, who wanted to establish a port on the mainland. The German East Africa Company challenged the Arabs in 1889 and took over Dar, making it the administrative capital of the German colony. The Germans laid out a grid street system, built the railway to Morogoro, connected the town to South Africa by overland telegraph, and laid underwater electricity cables to Zanzibar. The city passed to British control in 1916 and by the 1950s it had grown into a modern city.

Today Dar es Salaam is a busy city of around two million people. There's an eclectic mix of Swahili, German, Asian and British culture and architecture, reflecting its colonial past and more recent history. Like most African cities, there are substantial contrasts between various sections of the city, from the busy central streets around the colourful Kariakoo Market, alive with the rhythm of African street life, to the tree-lined boulevards of the government and diplomatic quarters to the north.

There aren't too many major tourist attractions, as such, but there's a lot of atmosphere to soak up. Life revolves around the huge harbour, where

traditionally-rigged dhows slip under the bows of huge cargo ships as they skillfully navigate the waters of the port. Well worth a look is the bustling fish market on the northern arm of the harbour. Every morning the dhows sail in to offload the night's catch, and yelling vendors sell an assortment of seafood, from giant crabs, lobsters and red snappers, to more unusual items such as bluefish and sea urchins.

It's rewarding to wander the streets around the Asian business district two blocks from the port, particularly along India Street and the intersecting Indira Ghandi Street. The business district fans out in a series of fascinating side roads and main streets. Here, the flavours and smells are of a little Bombay, rather than of Africa. You'll find everything imaginable for sale, from plastic buckets to three-piece suites, though you won't find many curios in the centre of the city.

Sights in the city centre include some interesting architecture – check out the German Hospital, the Lutheran Church and St Joseph's Cathedral. You can also visit the botanical gardens and the National Museum, where archaeology buffs can see the skull of 'Nutcracker Man' that was unearthed in the Olduvai Gorge (see p113). There are also exhibits on the Zanzibar slave trade and some memorabilia from the First World War.

Outside the city, there are some fabulous beaches at Oyster Bay – also the location of the

1&2 Dar es Salaam Fish Market.
3 Giant palm trees on a Dar es Salaam beach.

upmarket shopping centres and restaurants. But, if you want to do a bit of sun worshipping, rather pay a day's entrance fee at one of the large hotels whose beaches are guarded, as the public beaches aren't generally safe for tourists.

If you'd rather go in search of souvenirs, then the Makonde craft market north of Dar is the best place to go for wood carvings and Tanzanian art.

Zanzibar

Zanzibar's real name is Unguja. It's part of the Zanzibar Archipelago, which includes the island of Pemba, 40 kilometres to the northeast, and 50 smaller – mostly uninhabited – islands in the surrounding waters. The population of the whole of the archipelago is around one million people. Most of them live on the main island of Unguja, and the majority of these in the capital, Stone Town.

Today, a walk through the narrow, twisting passageways of Stone Town reveals veiled women with hennaed hands and feet haggling for coconuts in markets filled with the aroma of many spices, while old men sit on crumbling walls as they drink *chai* (tea) and gossip idly. The nineteenth-century Arabic buildings built from coral rag are testament to the time of the Omani sultans, who founded their empires on the spoils of ivory and slaves. Recently, many of the buildings have been restored to their former glory thanks to Stone Town being declared a World Heritage Site. They should be visited, if only to marvel at their elaborate balconies and carved, brass-studded doors.

Also from Stone Town, there's the opportunity to meet a 100-year-old giant tortoise on Prison Island, or book yourself onto a spice tour, which will inform you about the 50 different spices and fruits that grow on the island – from cinnamon and cloves, to jackfruit and sugarcane.

Zanzibar is easy to get around, whether on a public bus, hired car or minibus, and it's not very big. You could race round the whole island in a day, but there is so much atmosphere and culture to absorb it deserves more time. The ease of Zanzibari

life is best experienced in the laid-back villages on the beautiful beaches on the north coast around Nungwi, and Jambiani on the east coast. Miles and miles of white sand, not yet lined with touristy hotels – just simple, family-run guesthouses and coconut villages where seaweed lies drying by the side of the road. The ocean offers warm, clear blue waters, excellent reefs for snorkelling and diving, fantastic deep-sea fishing, water sports and the rare opportunity to swim with dolphins.

Inland, Jozani Forest is Zanzibar's only protected reserve, and one of the few places in Africa where the red colobus monkey can be found. Community guides can take you primate spotting, and the reserve is well worth supporting to help protect this endangered animal. Finally, Zanzibar is a seafood lover's paradise. Numerous restaurants offer the freshest catch from game fish to giant lobster. Alternatively, join the locals for dinner at the nightly fish market in the Forodhani Gardens on Stone Town's waterfront where a collection of stalls serve up freshly cooked seafood and snacks – fast food Zanzibar style. Everything is cooked over charcoal burners and the stalls are lit by gas lanterns. Here you can munch on a crab claw, a tiger prawn, a piece of fried red snapper, fresh lobster, kebabs, stuffed chapattis, roasted cashews and fresh sugarcane juice. It's a great experience and a fun and vibrant place to wander around on a balmy evening.

ZANZIBAR'S HISTORY

Over the centuries, Zanzibar has attracted the attention of many international visitors. The Persians, Arabs, Chinese and Indians arrived from the eighth century in dhows carried by the seasonal monsoons that blow across the Indian Ocean. With them they brought various goods, such as beads and cloth, to trade for tortoise-shell, ebony and ivory, spices, rhino-horn, leopard skins and later, slaves. (The name 'Zanzibar' originated during this time, and comes from the Persian '*Zendji-Bar*', which means 'land of blacks'.) It's thanks to the interaction of all these cultures that

1 The azure Indian Ocean around Zanzibar protects a number of coral reefs.
2 Exploring Zanzibar's islands by traditional dhow.
3 Coconut seller in the back streets of Stone Town.
4 White-sailed dhows have plied the East African coast for centuries.
5 Zanzibar is the perfect destination for snorkelling and scuba diving.
6 Stone Town is one of the oldest settlements on the coast.
7 Fisherman at Nungwi on the north coast of Zanzibar.

the unique coastal Swahili culture and language were formed. The Swahili people also adopted the Arabian religion, and today 97 percent of all Zanzibaris are Muslim. The oldest building on Zanzibar is the Kizimkazi mosque which dates back to 1107 AD.

Vasco da Gama was the first European explorer to arrive on the East Coast of Africa, on his way to India in 1499. He was followed closely by his native Portuguese people, who ruled Zanzibar from the fifteenth century to the end of the seventeenth century, when Arabs from Oman managed to regain possession of the entire East Africa region. They transferred their capital from Muscat to Zanzibar in 1832, and controlled the mainland coast from present-day Mozambique to Somalia for the next 30 years. They sent slaves back to Oman to work on date plantations and sold slaves destined for the East Indies to the Dutch, who were increasingly plying the coast. Approximately 600 000 slaves were sold through Zanzibar's markets between 1830 and 1873.

Cloves were introduced to Zanzibar and by the mid-nineteenth century, Zanzibar had become the world's largest supplier of cloves. Other spices, such as pepper, ginger, cumin, and cinnamon were introduced. Spices, ivory and slaves brought great wealth, and for a time Zanzibar was Africa's most prosperous port. This is reflected in the fine buildings and palaces still seen in Stone Town today.

In 1861, Zanzibar separated from Oman and became an independent sultanate. This left the door wide open for the arrival of the British, who were embroiled in the Scramble for Africa.

> "Zanzibar is listed in the Guinness Book of World Records for having had the Shortest War in History…"

Zanzibar is listed in the Guinness Book of World Records for having had the Shortest War in History as, when the British attacked in 1896, it took them only 40 minutes to seize control of the island. Zanzibar became a British protectorate in 1890. The British immediately proceeded to curtail the slave trade. They did not have great success though and slaving continued illegally until the First World War.

Britain began to break up its empire after the Second World War and by 1963 Zanzibar had become independent. It was only one year later, however, that the new government was overthrown by a violent revolution. The long-established Arab ruling class was overthrown and the government was replaced with Africans – the majority of Zanzibar's population. A declaration of unity was signed in 1964 between Tanganyika on the mainland and Zanzibar, and the new country was named Tanzania – a combination of the two names. Although they are united, Zanzibar remains separate from Tanzania in many respects, and today is semi-autonomous.

Stone Town

Stone Town is the old city and cultural heart of Zanzibar, where little has changed for hundreds of years. It's a delightful place of narrow alleys, crumbling mosques and grand Arab houses with their imposing, brass-studded wooden doors. Most of the buildings were built by the Omani sultans in the nineteenth century when Zanzibar was one of the most important trading centres in the Indian Ocean. European influences such as balconies and verandahs were added some years later. A common feature is the *baraza* – a long, stone bench built along the outside wall of a house. They also serve as raised walkways when Stone Town gets flooded in the rainy season. The walls of the houses are made from coralline rock, which is a good building material but erodes easily. Many of Stone Town's 1 900 houses have crumbled beyond repair, whilst others have been beautifully

renovated. Since Stone Town was deservedly declared a World Heritage Site by UNESCO in 2000, the Stone Town Conservation Authority has been working towards restoring the ancient town before these buildings are lost forever. The former Nasur Nur Mohamed Dispensary and the House of Wonders are superb examples of how imposing this type of architecture can look after a little tender loving care.

The best way to explore Stone Town is to walk through the fascinating network of alleyways full of shops and stalls selling spices, coconuts, mangos and lots of fresh seafood. It's a good place to pick up souvenirs such as jewellery, colourful clothes, beaded leather shoes and wood carvings.

The Arab Fort was built between 1698 and 1701 by the Omani sultans as the town garrison. The enormous carved entrance door formerly belonged to a wealthy sultan's house. The Portuguese then used the building as a church, it was later used as a prison and army barracks,

and today it's a shopping centre. The House of Wonders is well worth a look for its grand scale and opulent architecture. Designed by a British marine engineer in 1870, it was the first building on Zanzibar to get electric lights, and the first in East Africa to have an elevator – hence the name. The House of Wonders is an enormous square building with broad galleries running along all four sides, and a clocktower perched on the roof. It was damaged in 1896 during the shortest war in history (*see p122*), and was later used by the British as administrative offices until the revolution in 1964. The building later became the headquarters for Zanzibar's leading political party. It's still one of the largest buildings in Zanzibar, and is now a museum.

The Anglican Cathedral was built in 1873 by the British over the old slave market. The cathedral's altar is in the exact position of a tree to which slaves were tied and then beaten. For a small tip, local residents will show you the underground

slave holding cells, which are an eerie sight. As a dedication to the people who fought against the slave trade, the cathedral has a stained-glass window dedicated to David Livingstone, who was instrumental in the abolition of the trade.

The Sultan's Palace was built in the late 1890s for members of the Sultan's family and his harem. Following the revolution in 1964, it was renamed the Peoples' Palace and was used by various political factions until it became a museum in 1994.

The Nasur Nur Mohamed Dispensary was built in 1887 by Thaira Thopen – Zanzibar's richest man at the time – to commemorate Queen Victoria's Silver Jubilee. It's one of the most imposing of Stone Town's buildings, with four grand storeys and wrap-around decorative balconies. It served as a dispensary in colonial times and today is the Stone Town Cultural Centre.

Livingstone's House was built around 1860 and was used by many missionaries and explorers as a starting point for expeditions into deepest, darkest Africa. Most notably, David Livingstone lived here before commencing his last journey to the mainland in 1866. The building has had many incarnations since then: among other things, it's been a laboratory for research into clove production, and is now home to the Zanzibar Tourist Office.

Prison Island

Prison Island is just off the coast of Stone Town and it's a quick 10-minute boat trip from the old town's waterfront – just negotiate for a ride with any of the waiting boats. The island is fringed by a lovely, white sandy beach and a small coral reef, making it ideal for a spot of snorkelling and sunbathing – you can hire masks and fins on your arrival.

The island, also known as Changuu, was first used by Arab slave merchants to detain unruly slaves. In 1890 the British built what is intended as a prison for Stone Town, but the building was never used for its intended purpose. It later became a quarantine station for Zanzibar, Kenya, Uganda

1 Watching sunset from the terrace of the Africa House Hotel.
2 Stone Town harbour.
3 Stone Town port.
4 Spice tour to the plantations outside of Stone Town.
5 Zanzibar beach.

1 Zanzibar is also known as the Spice Island for the variety of spices grown around the islands.
2 Boy climbing palm tree to pick coconuts.
3 Local fishermen on a dhow.
4–7 On the north coast around Nungwi are some idyllic rustic resorts built from thatch and local materials. Here is one of the best beaches on Zanzibar, where the crystal clear ocean is perfect for snorkelling and diving.

and Tanganyika. Today, Prison Island is known for its excellent views of Stone Town and its giant tortoises, which were imported from Aldabra in the Seychelles in the late nineteenth century. They stand a staggering one metre high and could feasibly be hundreds of years old.

Spice tour

Over the centuries, Zanzibar's cloves, nutmeg, cinnamon, pepper and many other spices lured the sultans of Oman across the Indian Ocean. Today, a spice tour will introduce you to most of Zanzibar's spices and fruits (depending on the season) and a few historical sites too – such as the old slave market, or a ruined sultan's palace. Most tours are by *dala-dala* (pick-up trucks converted into buses) and include delicious lunches of seafood or Zanzibar curry, coconut milk, and plenty of fresh fruit. The exotic spices and fruits are grown in the plantations just outside Stone Town and there's ample opportunity to dazzle the senses as you taste, smell, and try to guess what they are. The guides give detailed descriptions of what the various plants are used for, though not all of them are for food. The leaves of the neem tree were once used as a cure for malaria

and indigestion, the iodine tree produces a sap used to fight infection, while the foaming berries of the unimaginatively named soap-berry tree were used for centuries as an alternative to soap. Other spices include ginger, vanilla, tamarind, del, menthol and cloves. The island was once the world's leading producer of cloves (three quarters of the total world supply) and the clove industry was the foundation of Zanzibar's golden age. The crushed leaves of the henna tree produce a dye used by women to decorate their hands and feet with elaborate, delicate patterns. On the tour you'll have the opportunity to get a body painting, but quick-drying Indian ink will be used instead, as henna takes all day to dry.

Jozani Forest

Most indigenous forests have been lost to agriculture or construction, but the Jozani Forest in the centre of Zanzibar has been declared a protected reserve. It covers 44 square kilometres (roughly three percent) of the whole island. The forest is 24 kilometres southeast of Stone Town – an easy stop en route to the beaches of the east coast. The reserve contains a large mangrove swamp and a tract of natural forest that is home to a few special species, including the red colobus monkey, Sykes monkey, bush babies, duikers, hyraxes, over 50 species of butterfly and 40 species of birds. The reserve is completely managed by the local people, who operate tree nurseries and act as rangers and guides. From the visitors' centre on the main road to the south, a knowledgeable guide can accompany you on a 45-minute nature trail into the peaceful, beautiful forest.

Northern beaches

No visit to Zanzibar is complete without some chill-out time on the beach, and one of Zanzibar's best beaches is at the mellow resort of Nungwi on the northern tip of the island. As it is one of the few areas without a coral reef, you can swim at all tides and don't have to walk out for miles to reach the sea, as you do on the east coast. The resort is little more than a collection of beach cottages, a short line of lively outdoor bars and restaurants, and a couple of dive schools, surrounded by banana palms, mangroves and coconut trees.

Most of Nungwi's cottages are built in a traditional African style with *makuti* thatched roofs to blend in with the natural surroundings. The bars are fantastically rustic and you'll find beautifully carved Zanzibar furniture standing right on the beach. Nungwi is a great place to relax, park off in a hammock with a good book and a cocktail, and enjoy the sun, sea and sand. The diving and snorkelling are excellent and it's worth visiting the turtle sanctuary, built by villagers to nurse turtles and other marine animals back to health before they're released into the warm waters of the Indian Ocean.

Nungwi is also the dhow-building capital of Zanzibar. It's a good place to see traditional craftsmen at work and watch the dhow fleets heading out to fish during the mid-afternoon. Reaching the beach is easy – simply arrange an inexpensive shuttle from Stone Town, or hire a car or motorbike. But be warned – the road to Nungwi is quite rough.

Eastern beaches

Another rough road takes you from Stone Town to the beaches on the eastern side of Zanzibar centred around Jambiani, Paje and Bwejuu. An extensive coral reef runs down the whole east coast of the island, protecting a long, idyllic sandy beach that runs for kilometres and must surely be one of Africa's most beautiful. The only problem is that the ocean is tidal, and during some parts of the day it's a very long walk over the tidal flats to reach the sea.

The local villages are linked by a rocky high street that stretches right up the coast. The local people make a living by farming seaweed and selling the octopus they catch. This is the place to eat fresh fish and seafood, and the best way to sample traditional Zanzibari cooking is to visit a local family's home for dinner. About two hours' walk from Jambiani is a large cave, containing a freshwater spring, in which it's thought that slaves were once kept. It's also a traditional shrine and local people come here to pray and make offerings.

At Bwejuu, the beach cottages are close to the Chwaka Bay mangrove swamps and a lagoon that offers superb snorkelling for crabs, starfish and sea cucumbers. Just keep your fins on, as the lagoon is a breeding ground for sea urchins and stone fish, both of which can cause painful injuries.

Mikumi National Park

Mikumi National Park is 283 kilometres south of Dar es Salaam in the Morogoro region. It was gazetted in 1964 during the construction of the Morogoro-Iringa highway. You will inevitably pass through it going overland from Dar es Salaam to Malawi, as this highway goes through the middle of the park.

Covering 3 230 square kilometres, Mikumi is bordered by the Uluguru Mountains in the north and the Rubeho Mountains to the southeast. The landscape is typical woodland and grassy plains, which are fed by the Mkata River flood plain, an area of lush vegetation that attracts a number

1–3 Zanzibar's beaches are pristine swathes of white sand backed by palm trees. Here the local people fish and harvest seaweed.

of animals throughout the year. These include lion, eland, hartebeest, buffalo, wildebeest, giraffe, zebra, hippo and elephant. Up to 300 species of birds stop over on migratory routes over Tanzania. The Mikumi forest elephants are much smaller than their big game park counterparts. They are mainly grazers so they do not cause as much damage to the trees. It's not unusual to see these elephants, and sometimes lion, from the main road, especially at night. It is only 50 kilometres from one side of the park to the other and the speed limit on the highway is reduced through the park because of the presence of wild animals.

4 The tiny settlement of Chalinze is at the junction of Tanzania's main road that runs from north to south and the turn off to Dar es Salaam. There's little more than a petrol station and a couple of shops, but the residents of Chalinze have tapped into the overland market in an ingenious way. All overland trucks pass through Chalinze on the way to and from Dar es Salaam and often stop to buy cool drinks. Young men here make and sell miniature metal overland trucks and each has been crafted exactly to copy the individual overland company's designs and colours.

5&6 Dhows have been used on the East African coast for centuries and are traditionally built entirely without nails, sewn together with coconut cord and pegged by wooden dowels. All dhows have eyes painted on the bows – for protection and to see dangerous rocks.

Page 130–131
The main highway that runs through southern Tanzania from Dar es Salaam to Malawi and Zambia neatly dissects the Mikumi National Park to the north of Iringa. It is possible to see animals from the side of the road, but animals have previously been the victims of road accidents, so it is important to drive slowly.

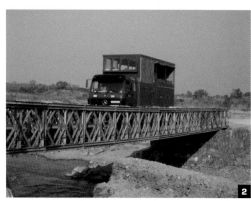

MALAWI

Malawi is a sliver of a country but, despite its small size, it offers a variety of attractions, most of which are well off the tourist trail. Overlanding is one of the best ways to explore the country, although the roads aren't the greatest and in the rainy season – which falls between November and March – floods can cause rivers to burst their banks, and bridges and roads sometimes get washed away. On overland trips between Kenya and the Cape, Malawi is roughly at the halfway mark, and it's a perfect destination to kick back on the beach for a few days and relax. The primary attraction here is Lake Malawi – an enormous freshwater inland sea. It lies at the southern end of the Great Rift Valley, and is the southernmost body of water in the series of lakes marking the valley's route south from the Red Sea.

When the explorer David Livingstone first laid eyes on Lake Malawi in 1859, he described it as a 'lake of stars', referring to its glittering surface. Lake Malawi is the ninth largest lake in the world. It's 560 kilometres long, 80 kilometres wide and 700 metres deep and forms most of the eastern border between Malawi and Mozambique. For such a large body of water, it is surprising that only one river, the Shire, drains from it. This eventually joins the Zambezi further south in Mozambique, before it spills into the Indian Ocean.

The lake covers almost a fifth of the country and provides a source of livelihood for many of the Malawian people. Fishermen, fish traders, canoe- and net-makers all ply their trades on its shores, and a common sight is that of a fisherman in his *bwato*, (dugout canoe), fishing on the calm waters at daybreak.

To the south, the Lake Malawi National Park is the world's first freshwater park and a UNESCO World Heritage Site. The lake contains a greater variety of endemic species of fish than any other lake on Earth. To date, World Wildlife Fund researchers have identified over 500 species not found anywhere else in the world. Most of these fish are in the cichlid family.

A number of tourist resorts and hotels have been established on the lake-shore. The more luxurious of these can be found on the southern shore, while on the northern shore are a number of rustic resorts and campsites close to the traditional villages. They are great places to enjoy watersports and most have equipment for snorkelling, water-skiing, paragliding, windsurfing and sailing.

Lake Malawi is widely recognised as one of the best freshwater diving destinations in the world. The conditions are safe, making this the ideal place to learn, and there are several dive schools at the water's edge. The lake is tideless, with numerous islands and rock formations beneath the surface, and the water is clear and warm, with temperatures averaging between 22 and 27 degrees Celsius.

Away from the lake-shore, there are magnificent plateaux, peaks and escarpments and the landscape covers a huge range of highs and lows – from the massive Mount Mulanje at 3 000 metres, to the Shire River depression at only 37 metres above sea level. Nyika Plateau National Park in the north is the largest of Malawi's parks. It continues into Zambian territory and is home to rolling highlands of dense evergreen woodlands and *dambos* (water meadows), that are the ideal habitat for leopard and many species of antelope.

Mount Mulanje, Malawi's highest mountain, dominates the extreme south of the country. Its rugged peaks offer wonderful views and top-class climbing and hiking. Tropical rainforests cover the ravines, where streams cascade from the high plateaux to the plains below.

"...one of the best freshwater diving destinations in the world."

The Zomba Plateau near the southern city of Blantyre is high and wet, with stunning views of the surrounding mountains, and there are some spectacular hiking trails through the orchid-studded pastures and forests at the top.

Describing themselves as 'the friendliest people in Africa', all of the Malawian ethnic groups live harmoniously together. Some elders attribute this to the legacy of the nineteenth-century Scottish missionary, David Livingstone, who arrived in Malawi in 1859 and encouraged tribal chiefs to work together to end the slave trade.

MALAWI'S HISTORY

Malawi was once called 'Maravi', meaning 'reflected light', perhaps referring to the brilliant glitter on Lake Malawi as the sun shines on its waters. Throughout history, people have been attracted to the region for its stable climate, regular rainfall and the ample supply of fish in the lake. For centuries, people lived here undisturbed in kingdoms governed by chiefs. However, this was before Arab and Portuguese slave traders penetrated central Africa in the eighteenth century.

Dr David Livingstone first set eyes on the great lake in 1859. By 1875, the Scottish Presbyterian Church had founded its first mission at Cape Maclear, followed by more European settlers who began to farm the land. With the growth of commerce and expanding plantations, Malawians migrated towards the settlers' farms in search of work, and towns and villages were established. Colonial domination became inevitable, and in 1891 the British Protectorate of Nyasaland was declared.

In 1953, the British federated Nyasaland with Northern and Southern Rhodesia (now Zambia and Zimbabwe respectively). But Nyasaland seceded ten years later, following elections won by Dr Hastings Banda's Malawi Congress Party. Nyasaland became independent from Britain in 1964 and was renamed Malawi. Two years later, Banda declared it a republic and one-party state. His regime was harsh and by 1971 he had declared himself President for Life. Any opponents were thrown into jail or out of the country. Some of his policies bordered on the bizarre: for example it was against the law for men to have long hair and for women to wear anything but skirts. Banda's foreign policy also attracted widespread criticism: he supported the apartheid regime in South Africa – the only black-ruled African state to do so. This cosy relationship with South Africa funded the construction of the new capital, Lilongwe (the capital had previously been at Blantyre), which opened for business in 1975.

4 Local villagers selling their wares to an overland truck.
5 Beach boats at Monkey Bay.
6 Malawian children especially love meeting visitors.

In 1992, Malawi experienced acute shortages of food because of poor harvests caused by drought, and the need to provide food for some one million refugees who had fled the war in Mozambique. People demanded change and by 1993 the ailing Banda was forced to concede. A referendum endorsed the transition to a multi-party democracy with a new constitution. While Banda was recovering from brain surgery in South Africa, elections held in 1994 were won by Dr Bakili Muluzi, who won a second term in the 1999 elections, but in 2004 Muluzi was replaced as president by Bingu wa Mutharika.

Malawi is one of the poorest counties on Earth and most of its ten million people rely on subsistence farming or fishing to survive. Drought and poor harvests in recent years have led to shortages in maize, the country's staple food. Malawi often has to look south to the richer nations for food aid. Despite this, the Malawian people are generally happy and friendly, and any traveller to Malawi will be made to feel most welcome.

THE OVERLAND ROUTE

From the north, entry into Malawi is at the border with Tanzania just north of the Malawian town of Karonga. There are two roads that follow the length of Malawi – one inland and one that follows the lake-shore. Most overlanders follow the shore road, as this provides access to the beach resorts. South of Karonga, at Chitimba, there is the option of walking or driving up the Livingstonia Escarpment that towers above the lake. It was here that Livingstone established a mission in the nine-

> "Positioned on a beautiful stretch of beach, and run with the permission of the local chief, Kande is a difficult place to leave."

teenth century, which can still be visited today. A dramatic switchback track leads up the escarpment and this is a challenging but worthwhile ascent on foot or by vehicle to enjoy the views.

Further south, Mzuzu is a likeable little town. It's a fast-growing administrative centre that provides facilities, such as banks and supermarkets, not generally found in the sparsely populated northern region. Most overlanders take the opportunity to stock up on provisions here.

Further south on the shore road are more rustic resorts around the quaint fishing settlement of Nkhata Bay and the village of Chinteche. Of these, Kande Beach is hugely popular with overland trucks and other travellers. Positioned on a beautiful stretch of beach, and run with the permission of the local chief, Kande has a relaxed, sociable atmosphere, making it a difficult place to leave. There are chalets and a campsite on the beach, a lively bar and restaurant, and the opportunity to go on village walks to meet the locals. Another highlight is a horse-riding trip, culminating in a bareback swim with the animals in the beautifully calm waters of Lake Malawi.

From the northern shore, most truck companies head for the capital Lilongwe, as the main road heads south from here to cross Zambia towards the Victoria Falls.

Those with their own vehicles can also explore the southern shore around Cape Maclear and the Lake Malawi National Park, which offers the best snorkelling and opportunities to see the lake's unusual fish.

This Page
1 Chitimba Beach campsite with the Livingstonia Escarpment rising behind it.
2&3 Cooking a pig or goat on the spit is a traditional overland experience.

Page 140–141

A storm gathers over Kande Beach on Lake Malawi's northern lake-shore.

Northern lake-shore

The northern shores of Lake Malawi are among the country's most beautiful and least visited. The north is much less populated and the beaches are more remote. Miles of pristine white sand are interspersed with jagged rock formations and charming fishing villages. It's also well within the tropics and the vegetation is greener and thicker, providing a dramatic backdrop to the lake. The lake is at its widest here, but on a clear day you can see Mozambique 80 kilometres away on the opposite side. Between Karonga and Salima, there are a number of simple beachside resorts where days are whiled away horse-riding along the sand, diving, or simply kicking back on the beach.

Away from the lake, the north is characterised by great highlands and tangled forests. Near Chitimba, the historic Livingstonia Mission can be visited by hiking up the Livingstonia Escarpment. Perched on top of a hair-raising road with 22 hairpin bends, the settlement resembles an English

village and was the mission post for the Church of Scotland in the nineteenth century. It was named in memory of the explorer David Livingstone. On the way are the Manchewe Falls, Malawi's highest, and a spectacular 50-metre drop with an intriguing cave behind it. The regional centre for the north is the small town of Mzuzu that sits on the junction of Malawi's lake-shore road and the main north-south highway (*see p138*).

Kande Beach

The Kande Beach campsite, 20 kilometres to the south of Chinteche on the northern lake-shore, is perhaps one of the most well-known overland stops in Africa. It was established in 1995 by overland expedition leader Dave Barton. Dave, from Nottingham, England, used the area for bush camping when he was running 'Trans Africa' overland tours. After being accepted by local Kande villagers, he suggested the beach could be a good way of making extra money for the community. The

chief of Kande thought this was a good idea and he suggested Dave start a campsite and employ the local people. Now, with his small army of workers and years of developing the site, he has proved to be a hit with the locals and has made one small village in Africa a better place to live. It is thanks to Dave's efforts and the donations of guests that a school and clinic have been established – a perfect example of how overlanding can benefit communities at grass roots level.

Southern lake-shore

The south shore of Lake Malawi has Malawi's greatest concentration of lodges and hotels between Mangochi and Monkey Bay. They vary from luxurious hotels with their own golf courses and airstrips, to simpler backpacker and camping spots. All have excellent, uncrowded beaches and offer a range of activities on the lake.

The village of Cape Maclear is the springboard for the Lake Malawi National Park. The park, covering an area of 88 square kilometers, includes the Khumba Peninsula, a portion of Lake Malawi and 12 islands. This part of the lake has been declared a World Heritage Site for the hundreds of species of tropical fish that are endemic to the lake. It's also the world's only freshwater national park and the fish are more abundant here than anywhere else in the lake. It's a favourite haunt for fish eagles and other birds such as cormorants, kingfishers and herons that patrol the water at different heights in search of their prey.

Lilongwe

Lilongwe has been the capital city of Malawi since 1975, when the capital was moved from Blantyre. It's situated in the fertile central region of the country and owes its status to Dr Hastings Banda, the country's first president, who was born just north of the town. It's very small for a capital city, with a population of only 250 000, but is useful for stocking up on provisions.

Lilongwe is split into two main centres a few kilometres apart, known as the New and Old Towns. The modern New Town is a collection of gleaming buildings with manicured lawns, where all the airline offices, travel agencies, government buildings, embassies, international aid agencies, banks, hotels and shopping malls are located.

The Old Town couldn't be more different. The original village of Lilongwe has bustling markets, bus stations, Asian shops and street vendors. A visit to the market on Malangalanga Road is worthwhile. It has the best display of fresh produce in Malawi – a limited resource in other regions of the country. There are also old Indian spice and cloth shops, and a big curio market outside the post office with probably the biggest selection of Malawi's famous traditional chairs. They have a broad back and the seat slips through this to form the back legs. This arrangement is completely adjustable, the reason being that in Malawi everyone sits outside in the sand. There are also colourful batiks, cane and raffia work, and every conceivable kind of wood carving for sale.

This Spread
1 Swimming bareback on horses at Kande Beach.
2 Overland groups have time to relax on the beach in Malawi.
3 Beach lodge at Chitimba with the Livingstonia Escarpment rising behind.
4 Outside bar at Kande Beach.
5 Beach on Lake Malawi's southern lake-shore.

ZAMBIA

Zambia remains unspoilt, unpackaged, and still relatively unexplored by the average traveller. A visit here gives you an authentic taste of what the whole of Africa once was like – wild, beautiful and unpredictable. This is a sprawling land studded with beautiful lakes, and filled with undulating plateaux of forest, savannah and marshland. The underlying crystalline rocks contain the bulk of Zambia's wealth in the form of minerals – the 150-kilometre-long corridor along the northwestern part of the country, known as the Copper Belt, is the mainstay of the economy. Zambia's other form of wealth lies in her 19 national parks and game reserves – their rivers and forests support great herds of game.

Zambia takes its name from the Zambezi River, which arises in the northwestern corner of the country and also forms its southern boundary.

The Zambezi, Kafue and Luangwa rivers form deep valleys, rapids and waterfalls – the most famous of the latter being Victoria Falls. Lake Tanganyika – the second deepest natural lake in the world – touches Zambia's northern borders, whilst along the southern border stretches Lake Kariba, the largest man-made lake in Africa.

The southernmost part of the country has two excellent tar-sealed roads that link Tanzania and Malawi with the Zambian capital Lusaka, which overlanders will pass through en route to the Victoria Falls.

All overlanders will eventually find themselves in Livingstone – once the colonial capital of the country – as it is the nearest settlement to the mighty Victoria Falls (see p152). Sharing the border between Zambia and Zimbabwe, the Victoria Falls are one of the world's seven natural wonders and a must-see on any visit to southern Africa.

Livingstone has some superb lodges, hotels and campsites, and has much more of an African feel to it than the modern town of Victoria Falls on the Zimbabwean side: goats roam the dusty streets, and colourful African markets and curio sellers are found amongst the faded colonial architecture.

The town is the centre of an incredible array of adventure activities focused on the Victoria Falls. The Zambezi offers outstanding canoeing upstream and white-water rafting and river-boarding downstream beneath the falls. The Bakota Gorge offers abseiling, rock climbing and hiking, or you can throw yourself into the gorge on a bungee jump, flying fox or gorge swing (see pp156 and 160).

An activity that requires absolutely no effort whatsoever – apart from the ability to lift your drinking arm – is the boat ride on the Zambezi to watch a breathtaking African sunset and admire the game on the river bank (see p164).

> "The Zambezi attracts magnificent game and the best way to view the wildlife is from a canoe – gliding silently up to a herd of elephant taking a bath is an enthralling experience."

ZAMBIA'S HISTORY

When Scottish doctor David Livingstone reached the Upper Zambezi in 1851, he 'discovered' and named the Victoria Falls, which the Kololo people had already called 'Mosi oa Tunya' – 'The Smoke that Thunders'. The people who lived right beside the falls and held them sacred also called them 'Shongwe', which means 'rainbow'.

After many more explorations of central Africa, Livingstone eventually died in a village near the southern shore of Zambia's Bangweulu Swamps in 1873. He was followed by agents of Cecil Rhodes's British South Africa Company (BSAC) in 1890, who signed treaties with several local leaders and proceeded to administer the region as Northern Rhodesia. Its capital was the town of Livingstone. (The seat of government was moved to Lusaka in 1935). Rhodes's ambition was to make Africa British from Cape to Cairo – hence the name of Lusaka's main street, Cairo Road. To obtain income, the BSAC imposed a Hut Tax on locals. The Livingstone to Ndola (in the DRC) railway was financed by this tax and those who objected or refused to pay met with harsh penalties: their huts were torched and their land handed over to white settlers.

The discovery of copper in the 1920s and 1930s soon made Zambia's Copper Belt one of the world's most concentrated mining areas. The BSAC, which owned the mineral rights, was to profit handsomely – 83 million pounds sterling by 1963. The mines required a large labour force and by the late 1930s, about 4 000 skilled European workers and some 20 000 Zambians worked in the Copper Belt. So many African workers in one place created a sense of unity that cut across tribal boundaries. This was eventually expressed in the state motto, 'One Zambia One Nation'.

In 1948, the African Mineworkers' Union was established. They staged several strikes to demonstrate against unfair taxes, poor working conditions and white rule. A 58-day strike in 1955 ended in victory for the miners, and the mining companies were forced to move Africans into managerial positions.

In 1958, young nationalists formed the United National Independence Party led by Kenneth Kaunda, which engaged in a continuous and largely peaceful campaign for independence. Elections were held in 1964, and Kaunda became president of the newly independent Zambia. But, independence was not a great success story. Kaunda remained in office for 27 years, controlling a one-party state. His attempts to 'decolonise' the economy by nationalising it resulted in inefficiency and corruption.

In 1990, there was a series of food riots and an attempted coup, and the demand for change became so urgent that Kaunda had to concede. The subsequent elections held in 1991 were won by the newly formed Movement for Multi-party Democracy, led by Frederick Chiluba, who became Zambia's second president.

Chiluba didn't do much better, however. He inherited an empty treasury, a foreign debt of seven-billion US dollars and a country of people who were poorer than they had been at independence in 1964. There was another coup attempt in 1997 and Chiluba declared a state of emergency, throwing numerous opposition leaders and military officers into jail. Then, in 2001, he tried to change the constitution to allow him to stand for a third term. After a public outcry he agreed to stand down. Chiluba named Levy Mwanawasa, who won that year's elections, as his successor. In a surprising turn of events, Mwanawasa impressed the country in early 2003 by removing Chiluba's presidential immunity and bringing him to trial on charges of corruption.

This Spread
1 The Smoke That Thunders.

THE OVERLAND ROUTE

Zambia is a big country to drive across. It's extremely rural and, as there are few campsites, it takes at least a couple of long driving days to get from one side of the country to the other. The distance from the Malawian border to Livingstone in the extreme southwest is a little over 1 000 kilometres, and further north, the Great North Road stretches some 1 500 kilometres from Tanzania to Livingstone.

The only worthy attraction on the overland route between these destinations is the South Luangwa National Park in the northeast, accessed from the northeastern town of Chipata, which is actually closer to Malawi's capital of Lilongwe than it is to Lusaka. South Luangwa is a truly wild park that receives very few visitors. It has one of the largest concentrations of leopard in Africa and is the stomping ground for thousands of elephant.

Further south, roughly midway between Malawi and Lusaka, the road crosses the Luangwa River over a rather impressive suspension bridge. To the south of here, the Luangwa flows into the mighty Zambezi.

Driving through Lusaka is fairly straightforward, although you should be aware of crime, as thefts from vehicles do happen. It is a useful stopover, though, as there are large supermarkets to the south of town and good campsites on outlying farms. The final leg to Livingstone is again on a good road, and another road leads south from Lusaka to Harare in Zimbabwe, if that's where you're headed. On the approach to Livingstone, look out for the spray from the Victoria Falls, which can sometimes be seen from several kilometres away.

From Livingstone there is the option of crossing the famous Victoria Falls Railway Bridge into Zimbabwe, or driving the 60 kilometres from Livingstone to the Kazungula ferry – a vehicle and passenger ferry that crosses the Zambezi to Namibia's Caprivi Strip. From here it is a short drive into Botswana.

1 The Kazungula Ferry across the Zambezi River.
2 Leopards are prolific in Zambia's game parks.

1 Lion.
2 Walking safari.
3 Crocodile.
4 Elephant.
5 Leopard.

South Luangwa National Park

Zambia's remote South Luangwa National Park is one of Africa's best-kept secrets. The now famous 'walking safari' originated here – there's nothing like being on foot in the African bush to sharpen the senses and heighten the wilderness experience.

The concentration of game around the Luangwa River and its lagoons is among the most intense in Africa. There's such an abundance of animals in this 9 050-square-kilometre park that it could almost be called crowded. The changing seasons add to the area's richness, as it evolves from dry, bare bushveld in winter, to a lush, green wonderland in the summer months.

The park is inhabited by 60 different animal species and over 400 species of birds. The only notable exclusion is the rhino, which has sadly been poached to extinction here. Antelope, wildebeest and zebra congregate on the open savannah grasslands, and are stalked by lion and the African hunting dog. The muddy Luangwa River is home to hundreds of crocodiles and you'll also come across large numbers of hippos – sometimes over 100 animals in a single pod. Enormous elephants can frequently be seen crossing the river's sand banks. On a night drive, you're quite likely to spot more unusual animals, such as the honey badger or civet cat, and the deep Luangwa forests provide the perfect habitat for leopard.

South Luangwa is inaccessible during the rainy season from December until about April, and most camps close over this time. The tracks turn to mud and even the access road to the park is impassable. May to August is drier and cool, while it gets very hot in September and October, when the earth becomes bone-dry. The animals congregate along the shrinking river and remaining waterholes, so these hot months are the best for game viewing. There are luxury lodges within the park and campsites near the entrance, overlooking the Luangwa River. These are great spots for sundowners while watching the animals drink.

"There's nothing like being on foot in the African bush to sharpen the senses and heighten the wilderness experience."

Lusaka

The overland route takes travellers through Zambia's capital, Lusaka – a sprawling, swollen city that has grown too fast and holds little appeal. Lusaka didn't exist before the twentieth century and until 1935, when the country's capital was moved here from Livingstone, it was just a sleepy agricultural village. There was rapid growth during the 1960s, and it's now one of the fastest-growing cities in central Africa, with a population of two million people.

Lusaka is characterised by high-rise concrete buildings and sprawling shanty towns. It is not the cleanest city in the world, and visitors should be aware that petty theft exists. But Lusaka is also undergoing a face-lift. New, modern shopping malls and smart fast-food outlets are being built, old buildings are being refurbished, and the potholes in the roads are being filled. To Zambia's villagers, Lusaka is a glittering place, and it draws rural Zambians in search of jobs and fulfilled dreams.

Livingstone

Livingstone owes its existence to the Victoria Falls and, as you may have guessed, was named after the missionary and explorer Dr David Livingstone – the first European to discover, name and tell the rest of world about the mighty falls.

The town was founded in 1905, after the completion of the railway bridge across the Zambezi, just below the Victoria Falls, to what is now Zimbabwe. Residents of an earlier riverside settlement, called Old Drift, moved to the new site beside the railway line – 11 kilometres upstream from the falls. Their move was inspired as a way of escaping the high prevalence of malaria on the mosquito-infested, swampy banks of the Zambezi.

Much of Livingstone's main street, Mosi-Oa-Tunya Road, is lined with jacaranda trees and colonial buildings. Many of these are more than 100 years old and, with their wide verandas and corrugated iron roofs, are typical of the town's English settler architecture.

1 Livingstone Street.
2&3 Both Livingstone and Victoria Falls on the Zimbabwe side are great places to pick up African curios. In Livingstone there is a craft market at the entrance gate of the Mosi-Oa-Tunya National Park, and at Victoria Falls a large market in the centre of town where you can also watch the craftspeople at work.

Although there is a certain air of neglect about it, Livingstone's colonial character and easygoing African charm make it a more interesting place to visit than the Zimbabwean town of Victoria Falls on the opposite side of the Zambezi – the latter is a victim of bad 1970s town planning. When Victoria Falls was first established, more visitors chose it as their base to view the falls but today, travellers prefer the Zambian side because of the ongoing political problems in Zimbabwe. Livingstone is been rejuvenated as a result. New hotels are being built along the river banks and houses in the town are being restored and opened as guest houses. The main road now boasts a number of eating and drinking venues and is once again full of safari vehicles and transfer buses.

Livingstone is a compact town and it's easy to get around here. There are a few interesting sights along Mosi-Oa-Tunya Road, including the Livingstone Museum, which houses memorabilia related to David Livingstone and his exploration of the region in the 1850s. The Railway Museum is also worth a look.

Other local attractions include the Mosi-Oa-Tunya (The Smoke that Thunders) National Park, adjacent to the Victoria Falls. Here, it's possible to book yourself onto a walking safari to track rhino (*see below*).

There are also a host of activities related to the falls, and many operate from the Zambian side of the Zambezi Bridge. In the Bakota Gorge, you can go white-water rafting and river-boarding on the rapids below the falls, or you can splash around in a powerful jet boat. You can throw yourself from the top on a gorge swing, flying fox or abseil (*see p160–161*). On the edge of town you'll find the airfield where helicopters and microlights depart for scenic flights over the falls.

Once you've done all this, you can simply walk over the bridge to Zimbabwe and try the activities available on that side (*see p178–183*). Don't forget to bungee jump off the bridge itself on the way. It's said that Zambia Railways makes more profit from the bungee jump, whose operators pay a fee to use the bridge, than they do from the whole of Zambia's rail network each year.

Mosi-Oa-Tunya National Park

Situated along the upper Zambezi, Mosi-Oa-Tunya stretches from, and includes, the Victoria Falls, for about 12 kilometres up river. Much of the park is covered by drought-resistant mopane woodland and tall riverine forest of large trees and ilala palms. It covers only 66 square kilometres but provides a home for numerous antelope, zebra, giraffe and several introduced rhino.

The Victoria Falls are 1.7 kilometres wide, with a vertical drop of over 100 metres, and the volume of water tumbling into the Bakota Gorge at the height of the rainy season is nine million litres per second. In the Mosi-Oa-Tunya National Park, you can walk right up to the edge of the falls – looking down on the thunderous waters, and feeling the spray on your face, is an unforgettable experience.

"Mosi-Oa-Tunya – smoke that thunders"

1 Aerial view of Victoria Falls.
2 Helicopter flight over the upper Zambezi River.
3 Microlight ride over a pod of hippo.
4 The best view of Victoria Falls is undoubtedly from the air.
5 Flights also go in search of game on the riverbanks.
6 The upper Zambezi River before it plunges over the Victoria Falls.
7 The famous Victoria Falls Railway Bridge that spans the Bakota Gorge between Zambia and Zimbabwe.

Another special vantage point is from the Knife Edge Bridge, which gives the best view of the main falls, the Eastern Cataract and the Boiling Pot, which is where the river turns and heads down the gorge. You may also spot people white-water rafting in the rapids below.

The Victoria Falls are at their most impressive after the wet season. Although the volume of water is much lower during the dry season, this is when you are able to walk along the lip of the falls and, if the water level is really low, make your way across to Livingstone Island, where David Livingstone had his first glimpse of the falls. For sheer madness, take a leap into the pool right at the top of the falls, which you'll have to find with the help of a guide. It's a thrilling experience to swim so close to a sheer drop, as the water surges into the gorge only metres away from you. Rest assured, the sight of you jumping into the water will definitely startle the people on the opposite side of the gorge in Zimbabwe.

It's also possible to view the falls at full moon. The park remains open in the evenings for this purpose, allowing visitors the opportunity to view a lunar rainbow.

Alternatively, experience an aerial view of the waters on a scenic flight from Livingstone by microlight or helicopter. This is the best way to appreciate the awesome power of the water as it surges into the zigzagging gorge below.

1–5 Preparation for the bungee jump takes place in the middle of the Victoria Falls Railway Bridge where the bungee platform is located on the side of the bridge. Here, the bungee masters attach the cord to your feet and put you in a harness, used to pull you back up to the bridge after the jump.

Bungee jumping

When you do the adrenalin-charged Victoria Falls bungee, be prepared to take a massive leap from the road and rail bridge spanning the Bakota Gorge, which lies in the no-man's-land between Zambia and Zimbabwe. At 111 metres, Victoria Falls was, until relatively recently, the highest bungee jump in the world. But the jump at the 216-metre-high Bloukrans Bridge on South Africa's Garden Route now holds the title.

This breathtaking feat, made even more memorable by the spectacular backdrop of the Victoria Falls, is hugely popular, and over 60 000 people have jumped so far – all safely. Standing on the lip of the bungee platform is truly terrifying – the fear is so intense that it grips every organ in your body and pickles your mind. Jumping off the platform takes all the courage you can muster. Then, for a few exhilarating seconds, you plummet towards the swirling waters of the Zambezi River below.

The sense of space and silence is like nothing you've ever experienced before, until the tug of the bungee cord as it reaches its optimum length pulls you back to reality. But, it's still not over. The jump is followed by a series of exhilarating bounces that take you on an incredible roller coaster ride in the Zambezi Gorge – the bridge comes careening back towards you, and again you fly without feeling the cord securing your feet.

Go on – five, four, three, two, one... bungee!

6–11 If you are going to throw yourself 111 metres down into a gorge, you want to have a record of it. Photographs and videos are available to buy as a souvenir of your bungee jump.

Pages 158-159
5, 4, 3, 2, 1…bungee!

This Spread
1 Flying fox.
2 Gorge swing.
3 Abseil.
4 Gorge swing over the Zambezi rapids below.

The Zambezi Swing

The Zambezi Swing has been set up across the top of the Bakota Gorge, and is the world's first cable gorge swing. Around 135 metres of cable spans the top of the 75-metre-high gorge, which has a sliding pulley system hanging from it. Once you've been firmly and securely attached in a full body harness, you take a running jump from a wooden platform and plunge for a heart-in-the-mouth 50 metres, before swinging out into the middle of the gorge. The jump ends with several thrilling pendulum swings before clients are lowered to the ground.

The flying fox is an alternative to the swing – a cable slide sends you coasting smoothly, at over 100 kilometres per hour, to the other side of the spectacular gorge.

Then there's the 53-metre abseil (backwards) or 'rap' jump (facing forward). A full-day trip includes the abseil, flying fox and as many gorge swings as you feel you can handle.

4

"The Victoria Falls, the brightest trinket in the globe-trotters box of curios." – William Plomer

White-water rafting & riverboarding

One of the most famous activities available at Victoria Falls is white-water rafting on the lower Zambezi. Considered one of the best stretches of commercially-run river in the world, the Zambezi is *the* place to go for some top-class grade five rafting. Adrenalin junkies can look forward to a wild roller coaster ride on the 23 foamy rapids, which stretch for 22 kilometres from the bottom of the Victoria Falls. Stairway to Heaven, Overland Truck Eater, and Oblivion are just a few of the names of these rapids, which are run in large, inflatable rubber rafts launched from just below the plunging falls.

There's also the option of getting kitted out with a wetsuit, life jacket, helmet and fins, and trying your hand at riverboarding. The main difference between riverboarding and white-water rafting is that, in the former activity, you are in charge of your own board on the river. The attraction is the physical freedom and the sense of achievement gained by tackling the mighty Zambezi on your own. Before starting out, you need to be confident and relaxed in the water, as well as a strong swimmer. Basic riverboarding skills are taught in still water, before boarders progress to the crashing

1–9 The Bakota Gorge below the Victoria Falls is one of the world's leading locations for first-class grade-five white-water adventure. Experience the turbulent rapids by raft or riverboard.

rapids. The experience of being punched through a turbulent rapid is a huge adrenalin rush, and boarders can also stop at 'play spots' along the way to surf and ride whirlpools and eddies.

For both rafting and boarding, low-water runs are the most adventurous and generally operate from the middle of August to late December, when the rapids are mostly grades four or five and all 23 are navigable. There is one grade six, which you have to walk around – only the experienced guides, or 'river gods', are permitted to steer rafts and kayaks through it. High-water runs only traverse rapids 11 to 18 from the beginning of July to mid-August – you're less likely to be spilt from the raft on these runs, so they appeal to the more timid and to those less confident of their abilities in the water.

The high, black cliffs of Bakota Gorge enclose some striking scenery, but remember that, at almost 100 metres deep, it's tough to walk out of this place. You'll definitely be glad of the cold beer waiting at the top of the gorge after a day of being thrown around in white water, followed by a very steep climb. Videos and still photographs are available for purchase as a souvenir of your wet and wild experience.

Sunset cruises

Every self-respecting overlander visiting Livingstone or Victoria Falls will book themselves onto a sunset or 'Booze Cruise' – a time-long tradition on the Zambezi River and the best way to celebrate being at the Victoria Falls. Open pontoons carrying chairs depart in the late afternoon and gently motor along the upper Zambezi, while the guide points out game. You will most certainly see hippos and perhaps crocodiles in the water and, if you are really lucky, you may spot elephant as they wade and swim from the mainland across to the many forested islands in the river. Giraffe and buffalo can often be spotted on the shore, and the riverbanks are a haven for birds.

But the real point of the Booze Cruise is to watch a brilliant sunset over the Zambezi with a sundowner in hand. You can drink and eat as much as you want to, so everyone on board is in a great party mood by the time the boat returns to the jetty after a few hours of fun spent on the water.

"Watch a brilliant sunset over the Zambezi with sundowner in hand."

1 Pontoon on the Zambezi.
2 Elephant-riding can be enjoyed on both the Zambian and Zimbabwean sides of the Victoria Falls. For more information see the Zimbabwe chapter.
3 Overland group on a booze cruise.

ZIMBABWE

Zimbabwe offers a generous cross-section of the Africa that all travellers want to see – exotic scenery, interesting cultures, and game parks full of magnificent wildlife. The Victoria Falls, where the Zambezi River spills dramatically into the Bakota Gorge, are the country's principal attraction. Zimbabwe is also the location of the oldest stone structure south of the Sahara. Africa's largest ancient stone monument after Egypt's pyramids is Great Zimbabwe, from which the nation takes its name. Situated in Masvingo, the Zimbabwe ruins, as they are commonly known, are a World Heritage Site and bear testimony to the history of this region as a home to ancient civilisations. The history of Great Zimbabwe is almost unfathomable – it's nearly 1 000 years old and was once home to 10 000 ancestors of the Shona people.

Zimbabwe is a land-locked country bordered by Zambia to the northwest, Mozambique to the northeast, South Africa to the south and Botswana to the southwest. The central highveld region is dotted with small hills and koppies (massive granite outcrops) and is the location of the two main cities, Harare and Bulawayo. The hills give rise to many rivers, which drain into the man-made Lake Kariba to the northwest, the marshes of Botswana to the west, or the Zambezi River to the northeast. The lowveld has the Limpopo Valley in the south and the Zambezi Valley in the north. Both are semi-arid bush where it gets extremely hot in summer. The eastern highlands, bordering Mozambique, include the fertile Chimanimani and Inyanga mountain ranges, where the misty green hills are of great scenic beauty.

The capital Harare, formerly Salisbury, is Zimbabwe's commercial and industrial centre and the location of the international airport, although international flights also arrive at Victoria Falls.

There's nothing much in terms of major attractions to keep you in Harare for long, but it's an attractive city with wide avenues lined with jacaranda trees. Bulawayo, Zimbabwe's second city, is home to some interesting museums and is close to Matobo National Park, which has one of the best-protected populations of black rhino in southern Africa. Piles of balancing granite rocks conceal ancient rock paintings, as well as the grave of Cecil John Rhodes (*see p186*).

More than 11 percent of Zimbabwe's land has been set aside as parks and game reserves, which cover a wide variety of environments and contain an enormously diverse collection of species. Hwange National Park covers the easternmost edge of the Kalahari and is Zimbabwe's largest park (*see p184*). It is home to a staggering number of elephants, which migrate to neighbouring Chobe National Park in Botswana. You can experience another aspect of the Zambezi on Lake Kariba, where the Kariba Dam has halted the course of the river and formed a lake with over 2 000

kilometres of isolated shorelines (*see p191*). These are guarded by enormous numbers of game and best enjoyed from the sunny decks of a houseboat. Further upstream from the lake, in the Mana Pools National Park, the Zambezi meanders through a wide valley with steep escarpments on either side, and splays into islands, channels and sandbanks flanked by forests of mahogany, wild figs, ebonies and baobabs.

Influenced by news of political unrest in Zimbabwe, potential travellers believe that a visit to the country is not viable. However, the country's political climate has little impact on the traveller. Zimbabwe's national parks are completely safe to visit as they are far from the cities where instability has occurred, and Victoria Falls is not near any farmland or trouble spots either. Despite having taken a bit of a knock over recent years, the infrastructure is still fairly good compared to what you'll find in many other African countries, and ordinary Zimbabweans are desperate for a revival in the tourism industry to bring much-needed foreign income into the country.

ZIMBABWE'S HISTORY

Zimbabwe has been populated since the Stone Age, and the ruins of Great Zimbabwe, dating back to the ancient African kingdom of Munhumutapa, testify to the advanced level of civilisation that existed before the Europeans arrived. Zimbabwe has long been home to the Shona people, who today make up about 80 percent of the population. In the 1830s, the region was thrown into turmoil by the northward migration of Ndebele people from South Africa, who enslaved the indigenous Shona until the end of that century.

The British, headed by Cecil John Rhodes, arrived in 1888. Rhodes controlled the British South Africa Company and his great goal was for all the land from the Cape to Cairo to belong to the British. (*Also see p147.*) While Rhodes's great railroad through Africa ultimately failed, he did, however, colonise this region as Rhodesia.

This Spread
1 Elephants next to the Zambezi.
2 Aerial view of the Victoria Falls.
3 When the river is full, 500 000 cubic metres of water a minute spill over the Victoria Falls.
4 Jet boat on the lower Zambezi.

Colonial activities were stronger here than in many other African countries. British mission houses and schools forced their values upon the African people, and local customs – even the playing of traditional music – were banned.

Zimbabwe's road to independence was long and rocky. The country became Southern Rhodesia in 1923, and in 1953 joined with Northern Rhodesia (now Zambia) and Nyasaland (now Malawi) to form the Central African Federation. A nationalist movement emerged to protest against the new federation. At the forefront was the Zimbabwe African People's Union (ZAPU), consisting mostly of Ndebele, led by Joshua Nkomo. It was soon joined on the political scene by the Zimbabwe African National Union (ZANU) – mostly Shona people – led by Ndabaningi Sithole.

After the collapse of the federation in 1963, both ZAPU and ZANU were banned and the majority of their leaders imprisoned. Relations between the white minority government, led by Ian Smith, and Britain soured over the government's treatment of black citizens. Under increasing pressure to change its ways, the white government declared independence from Britain in 1965. United Nations sanctions against Rhodesia followed in 1968. Both ZAPU and ZANU began campaigns of guerrilla warfare from their bases in Zambia and Mozambique, and by 1972 the situation had escalated into a fully-fledged civil war.

The arrival of independence in Angola and Mozambique in 1975 put more pressure on Smith to accept majority rule. He eventually conceded and released the imprisoned nationalist leaders. Talks led to an agreement known as the Internal Settlement. Finally, in 1979 under the Lancaster House agreement, its legal status as the British colony of Southern Rhodesia was restored in preparation for free elections and independence. Elections were held with 53 out of the 80 seats going to ZANU black leaders. Robert Mugabe became president, and the capital Salisbury was renamed

Harare. In 1980, the independence ceremony was attended by Britain's Prince Charles and the singer Bob Marley, who wrote and performed a special song entitled 'Zimbabwe'.

However, the independent government has been far from successful. Almost immediately there was bitter rivalry between ZAPU and ZANU, and from 1982 to 1983 the North Korean-trained Fifth Brigade, composed mostly of Shona, was sent by the government to Matabeleland where they massacred between 2 000 and 8 000 Ndebele civilians. No one has ever been prosecuted for these massacres and commanders who perpetrated them are now at high levels in the Zimbabwe armed forces. Nkomo (ZAPU) left for exile in Britain, but returned in 1988 when talks led to the merging of the two rival parties as ZANU-PF.

From the early 1990s, Mugabe has moved to increase his grip on power and eliminate opposition, and his government has been riddled with economic mismanagement and corruption. Along with all this, there's been the forced removal of white farmers in a land redistribution programme that's led to the destruction of much of Zimbabwe's agricultural base. Over 100 000 farmers, farm workers and their families have lost their homes and jobs.

It was only a matter of time before organised opposition re-emerged. At the beginning of 1999, the Movement for Democratic Change (MDC) was formed. Led by Morgan Tsvangirai,

"In 1980, the independence ceremony was attended by Britain's Prince Charles and the singer Bob Marley, who wrote and performed a special song entitled 'Zimbabwe'."

the party pitted itself against ZANU-PF in the 2002 elections. Surprisingly, ZANU-PF won the controversial election. However, it was considered far from free and fair, and it is alleged that violence and intimidation were used in anti-Mugabe strongholds to prevent citizens from voting. The election in 2005 had a similar outcome.

Following claims of human rights abuses and election rigging, Zimbabwe was temporarily suspended from the Commonwealth of Nations in 2002. Mugabe retaliated by withdrawing his country from the Commonwealth altogether. Predictably, the situation has caused considerable economic havoc: fuel shortages, rampant inflation, and an increase in crime, especially around Harare.

THE OVERLAND ROUTE

On the classic Kenya to the Cape overland route, most overlanders will visit Victoria Falls from either Livingstone on the Zambian side (*see p152*) or the town of Victoria Falls on the Zimbabwean side (*see p174*). In Victoria Falls, there are excellent campsites, including the main rest camp that dominates the middle of town – the superb facilities make this an ideal place for overlanders to park up for a few days and enjoy the activities centred around the falls. Apart from the main attraction, Victoria Falls is simply a great place for weary overlanders to take a break from driving and enjoy the good restaurants and nightlife, curio markets, swimming pools, shops,

This Spread
1 Overlanders need to ensure they are topped up with fuel before entering Zimbabwe.
2&3 Zimbabwe's roads are in fairly good condition, but in recent years, like the rest of the country's infrastructure, there has been little maintenance.

Internet cafés, as well as local attractions such as a crocodile farm and casino.

It's also possible to take in more of Zimbabwe if travelling overland between Victoria Falls and the start/finish destination of Johannesburg in South Africa. On this route is Hwange National Park. Situated off the road between Victoria Falls and Bulawayo, the park is known for its abundant elephants and strategic network of waterholes providing excellent game-viewing opportunities. Bulawayo itself has an interesting line of museums and art galleries and is a pleasant city to explore, also featuring an excellent municipal campsite. Less than 50 kilometres from the city is Matobo National Park, an important sanctuary for rhino

and birds, and the site of ancient San rock art and the grave of Cecil John Rhodes. To the east of Bulawayo, near the town of Masvingo, is another important historical site. Great Zimbabwe, with its strange, conical towers, is the remains of an ancient city that was home to one of southern Africa's first civilisations.

Midway between Bulawayo and Harare, near the town of Gweru, is the location of one of Zimbabwe's wildlife success stories. The Antelope Park is not only home to antelope, but elephant and lion as well. There's an idyllic overlanders' campsite and a number of unusual activities are available, such as walking with lion cubs or swimming with elephants.

Pages 172–173
Buffalo and elephant on an island in the Zambezi river, Mana Pools National Park.

To the north of Zimbabwe on the border with Zambia is one of the largest man-made lakes in the world – Lake Kariba. Here, the Zambezi fans out into a vast inland sea edged with inlets and islands that are inhabited by a variety of game.

Driving in Zimbabwe is fairly easy and the roads are good, although there have been well-publicised shortages of fuel in recent years. From Victoria Falls, most overland tours cross into neighbouring Botswana at the Kasane border 70 kilometres to the west, which provides easy access to the Chobe National Park.

Victoria Falls

The town of Victoria Falls, affectionately abbreviated to Vic Falls by anyone who's ever been there, lies within the Victoria Falls National Park, just a kilometre or so from the great falls themselves. Still essentially a village carved out of the African bush, Vic Falls is home to a seemingly endless variety of adventure sports. Bungee jumping off the railway bridge that spans the border with Zambia, and white-water rafting through the Bakota Gorge downstream of the falls are just two of the most obvious attractions. (*See p156–163 in the Zambia chapter for more details.*) Canoeing on the upper Zambezi is also a magical experience that'll bring you much closer to nature. You'll have the time to enjoy the wonderful birdlife and varied vegetation, and silently to watch the animals come down to the water to drink and play. Horse-riding alongside the game is a great way to interact with the animals. You could even opt to amble through the bush on the back of a majestic elephant.

But, perhaps best of all is the constant lure of

1 White-water rafting beneath the Victoria Falls.
2 Old Rhodesia Railways carriage.
3 Victoria Falls.

"Once the travel bug bites, there is no known antidote, and I know that I shall be happily infected until the end of my life." – Michael Palin

4 Statue of David Livingstone in Victoria Falls National Park.
5 The view from Zimbabwe looks directly at the falls across the Bakota Gorge.
6 Bird's-eye view of the thunderous gorge.

the falls. From the entrance to the Victoria Falls National Park, located just before the railway bridge bordering Zambia, a network of trails leads through the rainforest surrounding 'The Smoke That Thunders'. Famous viewing points include the Devil's Cataract at the western end of the chasm, where a statue honours David Livingstone, and the heart-stopping view from Danger Point.

The town of Victoria Falls grew to meet the demands of increasing numbers of visitors to the falls and nearby national parks. David Livingstone's fantastic stories about the falls attracted many European adventurers and travellers to this once remote place. In the late nineteenth century, it resembled an American frontier town, with its bars, stores and gambling dens. Despite an outbreak of malaria and blackwater fever that briefly turned Victoria Falls into a ghost town, it continued to grow through the twentieth century. The bridge across the gorge was built in 1902 as part of Cecil John Rhodes's ambitious – but never realised – Cape to Cairo railway.

The town boasts some fine examples of Edwardian architecture, including the elegant Victoria Falls Hotel, built in 1905, and the Victoria Falls Station, where the Bulawayo–Victoria Falls train arrives. One of the 'must-do' Vic Falls experiences is taking high tea at the Victoria Falls Hotel on the lovely terrace, from where you can see the bridge and its bungee jumpers.

The town has a village atmosphere centred on the commercial district, which is dotted with souvenir shops, tour operators, restaurants and an African-style curio market. By far the best eating experience is at The Boma at the Victoria Falls Safari Lodge. This is a sumptuous all-you-

can-eat African feast, beginning with sorghum beer served in a traditional tin cup, followed by starters such as crocodile tail or ostrich paté. Then take your pick from the huge buffet of every kind of game meat imaginable – and some you can't. Mopani worms are eaten all over Zimbabwe, and if you dare to try one, you'll be given a certificate. There are shows of traditional dancing throughout the evening, and you'll also be given the chance to have a witchdoctor throw and read the bones for you. For late-night drinking, the Explorer's Bar is a Vic Falls institution frequented by rafters, or 'river gods', as they prefer to think of themselves.

The Victoria Falls National Park

The Victoria Falls are one of the seven natural wonders of the world. They are a spectacular sight and a must-see destination on any overland trip to southern Africa. David Livingstone named them for his queen, and noted in his diary that 'scenes so lovely must have been gazed upon by angels in their flight'.

The park entrance is a short distance down the hill from the town, as you head towards the border with Zambia and the famous Victoria Falls Railway Bridge. On the Zimbabwean side you look directly across at the falls, but when in Zambia you see them from the same side. Both views are worth seeing, so if you've got time, nip across the border.

The Victoria Falls thunder over a wide basalt cliff, transforming the Zambezi from a placid river into a torrent of rapids cutting through eight kilometres of dramatic gorges. When the river is at its lowest between August and November, as little as 20 000 cubic metres per minute flow over the lip of the falls. This is the best time for white-water rafting, as the river is at its lowest and therefore most turbulent. But, when the Zambezi is raging in April and May, as many as 500 000 cubic metres a minute smash down into the Devil's Cataract below, and the falls are obscured by heavy spray before the water powers

Pages 176–178
The Victoria Falls are
one of the world's seven
natural wonders.

through the Bakota Gorge. The views at this time of year are magnificent.

There are a number of activities centred around the falls and the gorge, including white-water rafting and abseiling, and Victoria Falls is without doubt the adrenalin capital of Africa. (See the Zambia chapter for those activities that operate from the Zambian side, for which transfers across the border are included.)

Canoeing

A canoeing safari on the calm waters of the upper Zambezi is a wonderful, leisurely way to enjoy the astonishingly beautiful scenery that lines the river banks. This part of the Zambezi is flanked by national parks on both sides and is a haven of small islands and sandbars, home to many birds and animals. Sit back in your comfortable two-person canoe and let the river carry you swiftly along.

Run the small rapids, explore the channels and inlets, and take in some game viewing. This is the quietest type of game watching there is, and sitting comfortably in an 18-foot canoe as you observe crocodiles slink from the sand banks into the water, is an unforgettable experience. There's plenty of opportunity for some close-up encounters with other wildlife, including elephant and buffalo, as they come to the water's edge to drink.

Expert guides accompany every trip, both for your safety and to provide a wealth of knowledge on the indigenous flora and fauna. Full-day, half-day, or overnight trips are on offer. For the latter, all camping, cooking and bedding equipment is carried in the canoes, and you spend the night on an isolated island.

Flights of the Angels

The greatest view of the Victoria Falls and the winding gorges of the Zambezi River is from the air. The best time to fly is when the spray is at its highest – from April to June, when the sheer volume of water creates spectacular rainbows. These breathtaking flights are often dubbed 'Flights of the Angels' after Livingstone's diarisied words (*see p175*).

Exciting flights in a small six-seater plane or in a helicopter that is able to swoop low over the falls offer a very special experience.

On the Zambian side, microlight pilots carry passengers in a harness beneath them, completely exposed to the elements.

This Spread
1 Canoe safari on the Zambezi River.
2 Flights over the falls can be taken by small plane, helicopter or microlight.
3 The best views of Victoria Falls are from the air.
4 Aerial sightseeing trips are often dubbed 'Flights of the Angels'.
5 Helicopters can fly through the spray of the Victoria Falls.

"Scenes so lovely, they must have been gazed upon by angels…"

"The best place to ride an elephant is, of course, Africa. It was previously thought that African elephants could not be ridden."

1–3 Elephant-riding is a rare opportunity to interact with Africa's largest animal and get an unusual perspective of the bush.

Elephant-riding

The best place to ride an elephant is, of course, in Africa. It was previously thought that African elephants could not be ridden, but thanks to some patient training, it is now possible to go for elephant-back walks in the bush. Such a trip is not just a ride on the largest animal in Africa, it's an unforgettable experience that enables riders to interact with the elephants while enjoying a ride through the wilderness. This trip-of-a-lifetime starts with an educational and safety talk, after which you are introduced to the elephants and their handlers. Getting onto the elephant involves climbing an elephant-height frame and hopping on behind the handler. The elephants amble through the bush for around two hours. Each elephant handler provides a wealth of knowledge about these magnificent mammals, and a qualified guide also accompanies your safari on foot. After the ride there is more interaction time with the elephants – you get to touch their tails or eyelashes!

Horse-riding

Another great way to experience the African bush is on horseback. You will be accompanied by a guide and tracker – both experienced horsemen who will bring you unbelievably close to the game,

4–6 The elephants and their handlers have a close and trusting relationship, and whilst being trained for riding, the elephants still live naturally in the bush.

4

5

6

including elephant, buffalo and antelope. Quite understandably, lion are avoided! Novice and experienced riders are taken on separate safaris. On longer rides you will explore the area above the Bakota Gorge, giving you a bird's-eye view of the Zambezi rapids below Victoria Falls. There are plenty of opportunities to canter or gallop alongside the antelope. Elephant sightings are frequent, wild dog may be seen during the rains, and python have been spotted. The experienced rides are challenging and you need to have ridden at least 20 to 30 times in the previous two years, and be able to be in complete control of your horse amongst the game.

Jet-boating

The jet-boat operation is a thrilling and relatively new adventure on the turbulent waters of the Bakota Gorge beneath the Victoria Falls. You'll never forget the feeling of having the wind in your hair and the spray on your face, as the powerful jet-boats speed through rapids, rush past gorge walls and wildly spin you around on the stretches of flat water.

Be one up on David Livingstone by experiencing a view beyond his wildest imagination – looking

1–3 A bungee jumper throws himself off the Victoria Falls Railway Bridge that spans the border between Zimbabwe and Zambia. See the Zambia chapter for more information about the bungee jump.
4 White-water rafting.

up at the awe-inspiring Victoria Falls from directly below. The jet boat ride will take you between the towering cliff faces of the gorge, under the historic railway bridge, to the Boiling Pot at the very foot of the falls.

White-water rafting & riverboarding

One of the most famous, adrenalin-filled activities available at Victoria Falls is white-water rafting on the lower Zambezi, which is famous as one of the best stretches of commercially-run river in the world. There is also the option to try riverboarding. Both activities operate from the Zimbabwean and Zambian sides of the falls. (*See the Zambia chapter, p163, for more details.*)

"...wildly spin you around on the stretches of flat water."

5–7 Jet-boating on the lower Zambezi provides unique views at the base of Victoria Falls.

1

Hwange National Park

Hwange National Park – in western Zimbabwe on the border with Botswana – is located on the edge of the sands of the Kalahari. It's Zimbabwe's largest national park and covers 14 000 square kilometres – the same size as Wales in the United Kingdom. The park is famous for its huge herds of up to 20 000 elephant that migrate across to Chobe National Park in Botswana, and is also home to the Big Five. One of the great things about visiting Hwange, is that, unlike in East Africa's game parks, it's very easy to escape the camera-happy throngs here.

Hwange came into being in the nineteenth century when the Great White Hunters arrived in the region. Their presence caused many animals to flee into the inhospitable western reaches of the country, close to the border with Botswana. The area was proclaimed a national park before the hunters could completely annihilate the remaining animals. The landscape in the park ranges from desert sands, to sparse woodland, as well as grasslands and granite outcrops supporting an abundance of game. Other than the Big Five, you'll find zebra, eland, kudu and giraffe, as well as wild dog, which, through the efforts of a dedicated team of experts, are once again breeding and growing in large numbers. Game is so plentiful that over 100 species of mammal have been recorded here, along with 400 species of birds.

The shallow pans threaded throughout the park make it easy to view the animals, especially during the spring months of September and October. During this desperately dry time of year, the area can appear very inhospitable to such a large number of animals. The pans are crusted and cracked, and the plains are yellow and parched. The park holds no permanent water sources, so 60 man-made waterholes with viewing platforms were introduced to sustain the animals through the dry season. Hwange is therefore one of the few African parks where game viewing is consistently good all year round.

Bulawayo

Bulawayo is the second biggest city in Zimbabwe after Harare. It was once a royal village – the seat of the Ndebele dynasty – until the British colonial take-over in the late nineteenth century. It's a laid-back, spacious and attractive city, with wide boulevards and a pleasing blend of colonial and modern architecture. The tree-lined streets and suburban lawns belie the fact that dusty Botswana is just over the border. Although Bulawayo has more than 600 000 residents, it doesn't feel that large and retains a wonderfully old-fashioned, small town charm. Weather aside, you could almost believe you're in an English country town 50 years ago!

There are several good museums which are worth a browse, many of which are housed in turn-of-the-century buildings. These include the Natural History Museum, the National Gallery, and the Bulawayo Railway Museum, where there are exhibits of railcars from the Rhodesian period, including the lavish private coach used by Cecil John Rhodes. He used this both in life and death, as it transported his body back to Bulawayo after he passed away in Cape Town in 1902. Rhodes is buried outside the city at Matobo National Park. Beyond the city limits, the Chipangali Wildlife Orphanage is well worth visiting. Orphaned, sick and injured animals, including big cats, are nursed back to health and cared for until they can be re-located to the country's national parks.

"Matobo was proclaimed a World Heritage Site."

1 Hwange National Park is home to large prides of lion.
2 Female kudu.
3 Male kudu.
4 Colonial architecture, Bulawayo.
5 Vulture.
6 Bulawayo street.

Matobo National Park

The visually spectacular landscape of granite outcrops at Matobo National Park, 50 kilometres from Bulawayo, was named 'Sindebele', meaning 'bald heads', by famous warrior Mzilikazi. This land is considered sacred ground, and amongst the cracks and crevices of the Matobo Hills is the Ndebele rain shrine to Mwari, the god of their ancestors.

The San, who lived in these hills some 2 000 years ago, also left behind a rich legacy in the form of hundreds of magnificent rock paintings. Matobo was therefore proclaimed a World Heritage Site in 2003 for having the highest concentration of rock art in southern African, as well as the highest concentration of Verreaux's (black) eagles in the world.

The national park also has a considerable population of both black and white rhino, which are best viewed on a walking safari, and other species of game include giraffe, zebra and various antelope. The park is especially known for its large numbers of birds of prey. Besides Verreaux's eagle, you can go in search of 32 other species of raptor.

The Matobo Hills are the final resting place of the controversial British imperialist Cecil John Rhodes, who requested that he be buried here. There are great views over the park from his gravesite – the area is aptly known as 'World's View'.

Antelope Park

Situated near Gweru, this park has the only campsite in the world where you can explore the surrounding area accompanied by friendly lion cubs. The youngsters roam freely and are only too happy to take a stroll with visitors through the African bush. The campsite, located on the banks of a beautiful dam, also offers the special experience of game viewing from the back of an elephant – and swimming in the dam with one of these magnificent beasts makes for truly unforgettable memories.

"This park has the only campsite in the world where you can explore the surrounding area accompanied by friendly lion cubs."

1–4 Surrounded by Zimbabwe's famous balancing rocks, World's View in Matobo National Park is the site of Cecil Rhodes's grave.

5–7 The Antelope Park offers the unique opportunity to walk with lions through the bush.

8&9 There are few places in the world where you can get this close to lion cubs.

10 Elephant-riding at the Antelope Park where the elephants will even take you for a swim in one of the local dams.

Pages 188–189
Herd of buffalo in
Matusadona National Park.

This Spread
1 House boats are a relaxing
way to explore Lake Kariba.
2 Petrified trees in Lake Kariba.
3 Kariba Dam wall.

"Sunsets are a distinctive
feature of Kariba."

Lake Kariba

Lake Kariba is an artificial inland sea that covers 282-square-kilometres of the Zambezi Valley. It is the continent's third largest dam, after Aswan on the Nile in Egypt, and Cahora Bassa, also on the Zambezi in neighbouring Mozambique.

Kariba was completed and the region flooded in 1955, which led to one of the biggest wildlife rescue missions ever staged, called Operation Noah. Over 5 000 animals were tracked, captured and relocated to save them from the rising waters. Today, the dam attracts vast quantities of game, both big and small. Huge Nile crocodiles inhabit the lake, as do many hippos, and it is not uncommon to stumble upon a herd of elephant on the lake shore or while walking through the bush.

Stunning sunsets are a distinctive feature of Kariba, as are the bleached skeletal trunks and bare branches of dead trees that were drowned in the dam all those years ago. They make excellent perches for fish eagles, cormorants and other water birds. The best and most relaxing way to see the lake is from a houseboat.

Matusadona National Park is situated on the southern shores of Lake Kariba. Here, a wall of mountains serve as a majestic backdrop to the numerous islands and fertile flood plains.

Kariba town is now a very popular resort with an airport, harbour, lakeside hotels and lodges, marinas, and watersports. It is also a commercial fishing centre and crane-like rigs for catching kapenta (sardine-like fish) illuminate the night-time waters of the lake.

Harare

Harare, Zimbabwe's capital and largest city, is located on the highveld in the middle of the country and has a population of around two million people. The name derives from the Shona word 'haarari', translated as 'one who does not sleep'. This is somewhat questionable, as Harare must be one of the sleepiest capital cities in Africa. It was laid out by the British settlers, and has many

4 Buffalo on the lake-shore.
5 Lake Kariba has many inlets that spill into the bush.
6 Statue of the river god *Nyaminyami* above the Kariba Dam wall.
7 House boat on the lake.
8 Harare.
9 Elephant at the lake-shore.

wide, tree-lined avenues, and plenty of parks and open spaces. The city centre is a mixture of aging concrete high-rises and turn-of-the-century court houses and government buildings. There are vast suburbs of large houses with manicured gardens that were built by white people over the last 60 years, though many have left Zimbabwe in recent years due to the political instability (*see p170*).

The National Gallery houses a display of Shona soft-stone carvings, and some of the original letters and notebooks of the early explorers can be seen in the National Archives. The National Botanical Garden has more than 900 species of wild trees and shrubs, and there are good views of the city from the Kopje, a granite hill rising above the southwest corner of central Harare.

BOTSWANA

Botswana is a largely roadless country full of savannahs, wetlands, deserts and wide open spaces that simply beg to be explored. With a population of only 1.5 million people in a country roughly the size of France, very little of Botswana is inhabited by humans and there are few urban areas. Her most remarkable feature is the Okavango Delta, a magnificent wetland fed by water from the Angolan highlands. In a doomed attempt to reach the sea, the Okavango River spills hopefully from the east, only to falter and die on the hot sands of the Kalahari. It forms the world's largest inland delta – a 15 000-square-kilometre maze of lagoons, secret waterways and palm-dotted islands. Here, sunny days are filled with the sounds of birds calling, hippos grunting and antelope rustling in the reeds, while nights are ruled by unseen predators.

TRANS - KAL
HIGHW

This is Africa in her most remote and natural state. Recognising this fact, Botswana's government has designated 17 percent of the country as national parks, with a further 20 percent as protected wilderness areas. The government has also taken a deliberate high-cost low-volume approach to tourism as a way of maintaining the country's natural assets in their most pristine state. This means that the country's safari experiences definitely don't come cheaply, but this eco-tourism policy has resulted in visitors being able to experience Africa at its most stunningly beautiful, and nowhere will you find yourself in a crowd of camera-wielding tourists.

"You can pitch a tent just about anywhere, including in some very scenic and isolated spots."

Botswana is the perfect destination for overlanders: the network of tarred roads is in excellent condition and there are many opportunities to go off-road into the wilderness regions. It's also a wonderful place for camping – you can pitch a tent just about anywhere, including in some very scenic and isolated spots.

The unspoilt Okavango is southern Africa's premier wilderness destination, and a visit here is *the* highlight on a trip to Botswana (*see p210*). The beautiful delta is a great place for special walking safaris, drifting along the peaceful channels in a canoe, or even flying over the lush water meadows in a small aeroplane.

On the eastern side of the delta lies the Moremi Wildlife Reserve, where large areas of dry land are interspersed between the wetlands. Here you can experience excellent savannah game viewing, as well as bird-watching on the lagoons.

But there's more to Botswana than the delta. Over two thirds of the country is covered by the mighty Kalahari Desert – sandy, flat scrub and thorn trees that are shared, not always harmoniously, between wildlife and cattle. Here are giant salt pans with eerily stark and endless landscapes that epitomise Botswana's reputation as being a land of wide open spaces.

In the northwest is the Chobe National Park, home to an estimated 120 000 elephant – the largest population in Africa (*see p201*). A boat cruise on the Chobe River, near the border town of Kasane, is the best way to see these animals drink their fill, and there's nothing more endearing than watching a baby elephant taking a bath. The park has an amazing variety of habitats, ranging from flood plains and acacia woodlands, to verdant flood grasslands and thickets bordering the river and supporting large concentrations of game. Venture further into the park by 4x4 to hunt for vast herds of buffalo, zebra and antelope.

It's not only the country's tourism policy that makes it unique amongst African nations – Botswana can also boast of having the continent's longest and most stable democracy. As the country has had no wars, military coups, or uprisings, the residents are peace-loving and friendly, and people of different cultures and religions live happily side by side. But, perhaps this is not so difficult given its large area (60 000 square kilometres) and tiny population (1.5 million). There's only an average of three humans per square kilometre – cattle and donkeys far outnumber people in Botswana.

Thanks to its abundance of diamonds, Botswana is also one of the richest countries in Africa. You can therefore expect to find an excellent working infrastructure and very high standards of accommodation and service.

BOTSWANA'S HISTORY

The first people to inhabit the empty Kalahari some 30 000 years ago were the San – also known as the Bushmen. They number only about 55 000 today, constituting a small but fascinating cultural minority in the country. From the fifteenth century the Tswana peoples began arriving from the south. By the eighteenth century, these people had established a powerful, highly structured society consisting of towns ruled by monarchs who controlled hunting, cattle-breeding and copper mining. The European missionaries who arrived in the early 1800s were very impressed with the orderliness and structure of society amongst the town-based Batswana (the collective term used to describe the Tswana peoples – today it's used to refer to any resident of Botswana).

The Zulu wars of the early 1800s produced a wave of northbound tribal migration, including into the area now known as Botswana. Meanwhile, the Boers began their Great Trek over the Vaal River, also crossing into the area and attempting to impose white rule on the inhabitants. By 1877, animosity had escalated to such a level that the British stepped in and the first Boer War erupted in the Transvaal. The Boers retreated further into the northern territory in 1882, prompting the Batswana leaders to ask for British protection. The British agreed and in 1885 they declared the area as a British protectorate known as Bechuanaland – today's Botswana. The southern territory became part of the Cape Colony and is now part of the North-West Province of South Africa. Bechuanaland was eventually brought under full British colonial control in 1890, when the British South Africa Company was established to supervise the whole region. (*See p147 and p169.*) Later, in 1909, Bechuanaland, along with Lesotho and Swaziland, declined to become included in the newly formed Union of South Africa.

Nationalism built during the 1950s and 1960s and as early as 1955 it had become apparent that Britain was preparing to release its colonial grip.

Following South Africa's Sharpeville Massacre of 1960, the Bechuanaland People's Party (BPP) was formed with full independence as its aim. Despite Bechuanaland being dependent on South Africa for food imports and on the wages of miners working in South Africa for income, the BPP opposed apartheid as well as Ian Smith's regime in neighbouring Rhodesia. In 1964, Britain accepted the BPP's proposals for the independent democratic self-government of the newly-named Botswana. The seat of government was moved from Mafikeng in South Africa to the new capital of Gaborone in 1965, and independence was achieved by 1966. Seretse Khama was the first president, who was subsequently re-elected until he died in office in 1980. He was succeeded by Ketumile Masire who was president from 1980 to 1998. The current president is Festus Mogae.

Botswana was economically transformed by the discovery of diamonds in 1967 – the diamond mines of Orapa, Letlhakane, and Jwaneng together make up one of the largest reserves of diamonds in the world. This mineral wealth has provided the country with enormous foreign currency reserves, pushing the pula to its position as one of Africa's strongest currencies.

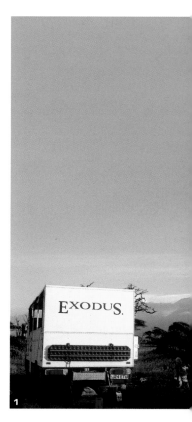

1&2 Bush camping in Botswana's wide open spaces.

Pages 198–199
Botswana is home to a staggering number of elephant that wander freely outside of the game reserves.

THE OVERLAND ROUTE

Botswana is located to the north of South Africa and is bordered to the west by Namibia and to the east by Zimbabwe. It is connected to Zambia by Namibia's skinny Caprivi Strip and here, at Kazungula, all four countries meet at a single point mid-stream in the Zambezi. When travelling southwards, most overlanders enter Botswana here, through either the road border with Zimbabwe or the ferry crossing from Zambia. This vehicle and passenger ferry crosses the Zambezi, allowing access to Botswana and Namibia from Zambia without having to go through Zimbabwe.

The Kazungula border crossings are both less than 80 kilometres from the Victoria Falls and it is logical to drive from the falls to Botswana's first highlight, Chobe National Park (*see opposite*). The park is situated just to the south of Kazungula near the small town of Kasane. There are several camp-sites on the banks of the Chobe River, and the park can be explored on 4x4 game drives. But the best way to see the wildlife is from a boat cruise on the Chobe River – a very relaxing way to see hippo in the shallows. (*Also see opposite and p202.*)

From Chobe, the road travels south to Nata, a small settlement with some petrol stations and

shops on the eastern side of the country. From the T-junction at Nata, one road continues to Francistown, where it splits again and goes north over the border of Zimbabwe to Bulawayo, and south to Botswana's capital of Gaborone. Here, there are several border crossings with South Africa and a highway to Johannesburg and Pretoria.

From Nata, the other road crosses the fringes of the Kalahari Desert and heads in an easterly direction to the town of Maun (*see p207*), beyond the Makgadikgadi Pans National Park (*see p203*). Maun is the gateway to the beautiful Okavango Delta. The Okavango River begins life in Angola, and when it reaches Botswana divides repeatedly into an intricate floodplain of thousands of channels that spread out into a broad, flat, inland delta. In the middle of the delta is Moremi Wildlife Reserve, the best place to spot larger game.

From Maun, there are a number of ways to explore the delta. Bigger overland vehicles such as trucks are not permitted, so most passengers take a two- to four-day excursion and are transferred by 4x4 or small plane to a bush camp or lodge, from where there's the opportunity to explore the waterways and islands by foot and by *mokoro* (dug-out canoe). There are several campsites in

This Spread
1 Botswana offers great opportunities for off-road driving.
2 Lion and elephant share a waterhole in Savuti.
3 Hippo in the Okavango Delta.
4 Crocodile.
5 Waterbuck.

"They drink, splash and enjoy muddy baths."

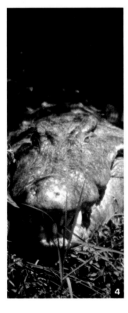

Maun where overland vehicles can be parked during this excursion. Independent overlanders can take their vehicles into the delta and stay at the public campsites in Moremi. The tracks consist of deep sand, so 4x4s are essential.

Back in Maun, there are two routes from Botswana to Namibia. The first heads north along a road that skirts the eastern fringes of the Okavango Delta to the Mohembo border post on Namibia's Caprivi Strip. The second road heads southwest across the Kalahari via the desert settlement of Ghanzi to the Buitepos border, which is 335 kilometres from Namibia's capital of Windhoek.

When you arrive in Botswana you may find that you are required to wipe your feet! At some of the border posts is a pit of disinfectant that vehicles must drive through, and all passengers must get out and wipe their shoes on a mat soaked in the same chemicals. The reason is that in the past Botswana's cattle have been threatened by foot-and-mouth disease, and this is just one method Botswana uses to combat the spread of the disease from other countries. The other method is the vet fences that criss-cross the country, localising the cattle (and foot-and-mouth disease in the event of an outbreak). You will undoubtedly cross these fences on any drive around Botswana. Again, vehicles are stopped and sometimes searched, and it is prohibited to carry uncooked meat and eggs, or any animal product, between the fences.

Chobe National Park

Situated in the northernmost corner of Botswana, the Chobe National Park fills the squat triangle formed by the country's borders with Namibia, Zambia, and Zimbabwe – and it's only 80 kilometres from Victoria Falls. A vast park of about 12 000 square kilometres, it has a great concentration of game and offers excellent safari experiences. The Chobe river frontage in the extreme northeast has lush plains and dense forest, whilst the central region has both arid pans and deep swamps. The famous Savuti corridor in the west leads to the Moremi Wildlife Reserve in the Okavango Delta. Chobe – Botswana's first national park – was declared as such in 1967.

The park's northern boundaries are marked by the Chobe River, as well as the border with Namibia. You can actually see the Namibian border guards at their look-out posts on the other side. The Chobe River rises in the northern Angolan highlands and, as with the Okavango and Zambezi, its course is affected by fault lines. One theory is that, millions of years ago these three flowed as one huge river across the middle of the Kalahari before joining the Limpopo River and emptying into the Indian Ocean. But it's thought that movements in the earth's crust split this flow into separate rivers, which now carry more water than all the other rivers in southern Africa.

"Chobe National Park is famous for having the largest continuous surviving elephant population in Africa…"

Chobe National Park is famous for having the largest continuous surviving elephant population in Africa, estimated at a staggering 120 000. Truly impressive herds gather during both the wet and dry seasons and, as regularly as clockwork, move along their well-worn paths to drink at the Chobe River. You can park amongst them and watch as they drink, splash and enjoy muddy baths.

One of the most popular safaris in the park is game viewing by boat and a 'must do' is to take an afternoon boat ride on a double-storey pontoon – gin and tonic in hand – to watch the elephants play in the water.

These elephants also migrate across the border to Hwange National Park in Zimbabwe, and are frequently spotted on the main road between Kasane and Maun. There are even signs along the road that warn of the presence of these gigantic animals.

Among the largest elephants in Africa, their ivory is brittle and they don't have big tusks – a fact that saved them from the poachers who decimated other populations in the 1970s and 1980s. Indeed, the elephant population has fared so well that it has placed massive pressure on the natural environment.

Herds of zebra can also be seen at the river's edge. Giraffe and warthog are common, while lion occur throughout the park but are most frequently spotted around the Savuti corridor in the west. It's not unusual to see hundreds of buffalo at a time, as well as wildebeest and zebra in their thousands – all closely stalked by predators.

Makgadikgadi Pans National Park

The Makgadikgadi Pans National Park covers 4 900 square kilometres and is located roughly halfway between Maun and Nata. The salt pans are all that remain of a once ancient super-lake formed some five million years ago, which covered much of northern Botswana and was fed by the Zambezi and Okavango rivers. The shimmering pans are the largest in the world and usually appear as an endless, glaringly white plain, which stretches to a limitless horizon.

During the dry season in this vast wilderness, the pans are hostile, salt-encrusted dust bowls. Only an occasional rocky outcrop and large, isolated sand dune interrupts the flat landscape. Palm trees grow in clusters on the edges of the pans and distinctive Baobab trees are dotted around.

The salt pans were once fed by the Boteti River, a broad waterway fed by waters drained from the Okavango Delta during the months of June and July. But the river gradually dwindled to a chain of pools, and then ceased flowing altogether in 1992. However, the stark landscape changes when the rains come – the pans fill up from mid-November and retain their water until the following April or May. This 'thirstland' changes into a great sheet of water, attracting many aquatic birds such as pelicans and flamingos. The transformation also triggers migrations of wildebeest and zebra, followed by predators including lion and cheetah.

The tracks are rough once you're off the main road, so it's essential to have a 4x4. You'll find two campsites overlooking the plains, where you can experience complete solitude, as well as the chance to go quad-biking across the pans.

1 Hippo yawning.
2 Elephant family.
3–5 Makgadikgadi is a vast flat area of glimmering white dust. Camping out here is a unique experience.

Baines' Baobabs

Baines' Baobabs were named after nineteenth-century painter and explorer Thomas Baines, a member of David Livingstone's expedition who painted a remarkable cluster of baobab trees in 1862 during his journeys through southern Africa. A prominent landmark, this grouping of trees stands on the pioneers' route to the swamps of the Okavango Delta. With their intricate branches towering majestically above the salt pans, they have supposedly not altered since the year in which Baines painted them.

The seven trees dominate a small island on the edge of the open, grassless Kudiakam Pan, which lies in the southern part of the Nxai Pan National Park – an extension of the Makgadikgadi Pans.

The area around Baines' Baobabs has three campsites. Though informal and undeveloped, they are great places for overlanders to spend the night.

This Spread
1 Baines' Baobabs.
2&3 The San (Bushmen) have lived in the Kalahari for thousands of years and may be the first humans to have occupied this region.
4 Children in Maun.
5 Herero women in traditional dress.

Maun

Maun was once a dusty little frontier town where local people brought their cattle to trade. Today, thanks to the popularity of the Okavango Delta and Moremi Wildlife Reserve, it's Botswana's tourism capital and the springboard for safaris into the 15 000-square-kilometre wilderness area. Maun is the base-camp for a thriving tourism industry that markets everything from horseback safaris to *mokoro* tours in the delta. There are countless safari and air-charter operations whose signs and offices line the dusty streets. In only a few years, the exceptional growth of tourism has turned Maun from a backwater into a booming town.

The name is derived from the San word '*maung*', meaning 'the place of short reeds'. The village began life in 1915 as the tribal capital of the Batswana people, and its reputation quickly grew as a rough-and-ready place of local cattle ranchers and professional hunters with a Wild West atmosphere. In 1920, Harry Riley built the first Riley's Hotel, which was then nothing more than a small bar catering for the men who arrived from Francistown – a gruelling 35-hour journey by horse and cart. Today, the hotel is still an important landmark in Maun.

With the growth of the tourism industry and the completion of the tar road from Nata in the early 1990s, Maun developed rapidly along the wide Thamalakane River into Botswana's third largest town. It's lost much of its old frontier town character and is now home to over 30 000 people who live in an eclectic mix of modern buildings and traditional huts. There are also shopping malls, banks, restaurants, a few hotels and some happening bars. Regular supplies of almost everything can be bought in Maun and the town services the various lodges in the delta, sending provisions in by truck or plane.

If you want to fly over the delta, this can be organised from Maun Airport – only a few minutes' walk from the town's main street. There are

1–4 The Okavango Delta is a vast wilderness area of tranquil streams, channels, islands and woodland. The best way to explore is on foot, by traditional dugout canoes known as *mekoro* (singular *mokoro*), and by flying over the delta for a bird's-eye view.·

several companies offering a one-hour sightseeing flip by six-seater plane. Pilots have the freedom to swoop low if there's something of interest in the breathtaking landscape below.

Maun has very few sights as such: lots of concrete, very few trees, and as the sun bounces off the white dust, it is blindingly bright. But the town still retains some of its rural atmosphere – it is surrounded by traditional domed, thatched huts, and you might see local tribesmen bring their cattle into town for sale, or the occasional indigenous red lechwe grazing alongside the donkeys and goats along the riverbanks.

Okavango Delta

Botswana's famous Okavango Delta is one of the world's last untamed wildernesses, and the labyrinth of lagoons and hidden channels covering an area of over 15 000 square kilometres is the largest inland delta in the world. Until the 1950s, local farmers referred to it as a 'useless swamp' and would have preferred the land to be drained and used as farmland. Its headwaters start in Angola's western highlands, with numerous tributaries joining to form the Cubango River, which then flows through Namibia where it's

called the Kavango, before finally entering Botswana as the Okavango.

Millions of years ago, the Okavango used to flow into a large inland lake called Lake Makgadikgadi, the remnants of which are the Makgadikgadi Pans (*see p203*), and on to the sea via the Limpopo River. These days, the river's changing web of channels flow one way this year, and another the next. Sometimes called a swamp, the Okavango is anything but that. It is mysterious, placid, and beautiful: an ever-expanding network of increasingly smaller channels hemmed in by reeds, linking islands and palm forests.

As the delta is so large, it's not always easy to spot the big animals and you'll have to look carefully. But rest assured, there are substantial populations of elephant, lion, giraffe, wild dog, leopard, cheetah and buffalo waiting to be discovered. There's also a full range of antelope, large and small – including the unusual red lechwe – and the delta is a veritable playground for hippos and crocs. Birdlife is prolific and varied, ranging from water birds to shy forest dwellers. With a menu of over 80 species of fish to choose from, it's a favourite haunt for the famous African fish eagle.

1 The well-watered Okavango supports large numbers of game, though animals can sometimes be difficult to spot in the long grasses.

The middle of the delta is protected by the Moremi Wildlife Reserve, which covers 4 890 square kilometres, or 20 percent of the greater delta area. The grasslands and acacia woodland here stay dry all year around and attract a number of the area's larger animals. Chief's Island is the largest landmass within Moremi and is flanked by the two largest rivers in the delta: the Boro and the Santantadibe. The dry, sandy interior of this 1 000-square-kilometre island is full of very tall mopane trees interspersed with clay pans. Elephant are numerous here, particularly during the dry season when they migrate from nearby Chobe National Park in search of water. Other wildlife include buffalo, giraffe, lion, leopard, cheetah, wild dog, hyena, jackal and a full range of antelope. The only free-roaming rhino in Botswana are those recently introduced to the Mombo area of Chief's Island. Wild dog, whose numbers are so rapidly dwindling elsewhere, are regularly sighted, and it is claimed that the Moremi contains about 30 percent of all living wild dog. Around the reserve are a number of long bridges, constructed entirely out of mopane poles, which rattle and shake as vehicles pass over them. These bridges are also used by the game to get onto the permanent higher ground and it's not uncommon to see lion strolling over them to cross a flood plain. There are three unfenced campsites in the reserve, and as the animals frequently hunt for prey at night, staying here will definitely make you feel that you are in the heart of wildest Africa.

The best way to explore is by *mokoro* or by foot. Excursions involve being transferred into the delta by 4x4 or plane to enjoy a couple of days drifting through the watery channels, many of which are brimming with water lilies. Your poler will always find a safe spot for you to swim, away from the jaws of the many hippos and crocs.

There's also the opportunity to go on an interesting walking safari with an experienced delta guide to track spoor. These guides are great experts on local birds, insects, and fish, as well as the intricate nature of the delta itself.

If you want to get the most out of an Okavango Delta excursion, it'll definitely help if you go in with the right attitude. Many people expect the delta to be teeming with game. It is, of course, but in reality the animals can be difficult to spot in the area's long grasses and tall trees. Rather regard the delta excursion as more of a general wilderness experience, giving you a wonderful opportunity to spend some time in a beautiful, peaceful and remote environment, in which the modern world seems a lifetime away. Then, if you do happen to witness a big pack of wild dog careering through your campsite one night, you'll be able to count this as a huge bonus on your trip of a lifetime.

"It is mysterious, placid, and beautiful: an ever-expanding network of increasingly smaller channels hemmed in by reeds, linking islands and palm forests."

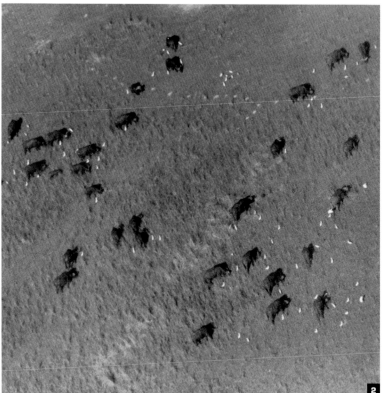

"Your poler will find you
a safe spot to swim
– away from the hippos
and crocs."

1 Exploring the Okavango by *mokoro*.
2 Aerial view of a buffalo herd.
3 Sunsets are a highlight of the delta.
4 Relaxing at camp.
5 Hippos are abundant in the shallow streams.
6 Polers steer the *mekoro* through the delta.
7 *Mekoro* silently glide through the watery channels.

NAMIBIA

Namibia is a country of extremes. It features a brutally hot climate, arid grasslands and barren red-sand deserts, and looks like no other part of Africa. It is a country of compelling beauty and wide horizons that offer a feeling of unconfined space, making this a hugely attractive travel destination. Namibia also has an excellent infrastructure with a large network of roads and some excellent campsites. Even the most remote places are accessible and it is a fantastic country to explore overland. There are about 5 000 kilometres of tarred roads and almost 40 000 kilometres of gravel or sand roads which are regularly graded and are usually well maintained. Generally, a 4x4 is not required for travelling in Namibia, though is necessary for drives through sand dunes, at the beach or in riverbeds. Some farm roads might also be difficult to negotiate.

Still relatively undiscovered compared to its southern African neighbours, Namibia's secret is its wealth of unusual landscapes that provide numerous opportunities for adventure. Namibia is one of the driest regions in Africa and gets very little rain, and the country is dominated by the brooding and desolate Namib Desert. Here are the highest sand dunes in the world, which march determinedly towards the sea in a dune field some 300 kilometres wide. A Namibia 'must-do' is to climb a giant dune at Sossusvlei in the Namib-Naukluft Park, the fourth largest national park in the world. The Namib is said to be the oldest desert in the world, where over time, the flora, fauna and insects have become adapted to their waterless environment. In contrast, hardly anything survives on the stark and inhospitable Skeleton Coast where both ancient and modern seafarers have met their watery end. Seals seem to like it well enough, though, and up to 80 000 make their home on the same rock at Cape Cross Seal Colony. Inland, Damaraland is well worth exploring for its beautiful scenery - tortured rock, open gravel plains and mounds of granite boulders, where there is the possible encounter with an elusive desert elephant. Sunsets belong to Namibia, and another must-do is to watch the sun drop over the immense Fish River Canyon, the second largest canyon in the world after the Grand Canyon. Jutting eastward into Angola, Zambia and Botswana, the finger-like Caprivi Strip in the north of the country is nothing like these arid landscapes, and is something of an oasis, well-watered and forested. To the west, the Etosha National Park is packed with game, and is home to a wide variety of species of birds and mammals that survive on the magical waterholes scattered throughout the park. Namibia is home to the largest population of cheetah still in existence and concerted efforts are being made to preserve the species in the wild. Namibia's wildlife sanctuaries give you the chance for some closer interaction – being licked by a cheetah is an experience not easily forgotten.

Originally inhabited by Bushmen, and later colonised by the Germans, Namibia, which gained its independence in 1990, retains elements of its colonial past. The German influence - their language, architecture and sense of structure - is still evident, particularly in the country's superior infrastructure. Even in its restaurants you won't have a problem finding an apple strudel or a flagon of beer. Windhoek, which means 'windy corner' in a local language, is the nation's modern capital. Its lacy network of small streets diffuses the gusts sweeping in off the Kalahari Desert. But it is the coastal town of Swakopmund that is Namibia's most atmospheric and interesting town. It's surrounded by sand and is today the location of a number of adventure activities, from sand-boarding to sky-diving.

Namibia is one of the least densely populated countries in the world. Just fewer than two million people live in an area of approximately 824 000 square kilometres – only slightly more than two people per square kilometre. But the diversity of its people creates a rich blend of cultures and traditions. The awesome-looking Himba in the north, with their gleaming red-ochre skin and elaborately braided hair, still live their nomadic existence and roam the desert with their large herds of cattle. In Bushmanland to the east, the old hunter-gather traditions of the San, the original inhabitants of southern African, are still being preserved.

Namibia is a very tourist-friendly country. It boasts clean, modern cities, a fully developed infrastructure, quality hotels and restaurants

"Namibia is one of the least densely populated countries in the world with only slightly more than two people per square kilometre."

and most importantly, friendly people. It is Africa for beginners, and travelling here is safe and hassle-free. Since it only gained independence in 1990, it also has one of the world's newest tourism industries and is one of the first countries in the world to include protection of the environment and sustainable utilisation of wildlife in its constitution. It's one of the few African countries to promote eco-tourism, and there are many initiatives that both care for the environment and involve local people.

NAMIBIA'S HISTORY

The first people to inhabit what is now Namibia were the San people, otherwise known as the Bushmen. They are hunter gatherers who roamed southern Africa's plains for thousands of years. There's still a population of around 27 000 living in Botswana and Namibia. In Namibia, you're likely to see them around the northern town of Rundu, though in the modern world they are struggling to retain their traditional lifestyle. The Namas and the Damaras came from the north from the twelfth century, pushing the Bushmen into the Kalahari Desert. They were followed by the Owambos and the Herero from the fourteenth century and

by the Ovambo in the early nineteenth century. Several kingdoms sprouted on both sides of the Kunene river.

The first European to arrive was a Portuguese sailor, Diego Cão, who briefly landed at Cape Cross in 1486. A few hundred years later, whilst the rest of the African continent was being carved up by the colonists, Namibia's treacherous coastline and the inhospitable Namib Desert constituted a formidable barrier. It effectively staved off potential colonisers until the mid-nineteenth century. German missionaries arrived in the 1840s and set about building carbon-copy settlements of their towns back home and introducing other idiosyncrasies such as Victorian-style clothing to the native people. Today Herero ladies can still be seen in the villages dressed in antiquated-style dresses with bustles and frills.

Meanwhile in 1878, the British annexed the natural deep harbour of Walvis Bay, and the area was incorporated into the Cape of Good Hope in 1884. A German trader, Adolf Lüderitz, claimed the surrounding region. Negotiations between the British and the Germans resulted in Germany controlling the whole coastal region, excluding Walvis Bay, which remained in British hands. The

This Page
1 Most of the landscape is flat arid scrub and there are few very high mountains. Much of the country is dominated by the Namib Desert that stretches along the coast, a natural extension of the Kalahari Desert further east.

German protectorate of South West Africa was established 1894, after a bizarre agreement. The British allowed Germany to add the Caprivi Strip to its territories (and thus get access to the Zambezi River) in exchange for Zanzibar and Heligoland, a remote island in the North Sea.

The next three decades of German rule were marked by bloody conflicts between the Europeans and the Africans, mainly the Herero. Between 1904 and 1907 around 60 000 local people were killed, many were ruthlessly driven into the Kalahari Desert to die and Germany introduced racial segregation. In 1908 diamonds were discovered near the coast, bringing a stampede of Europeans to the newly established diamond towns such as Lüderitz, which for a few years in the 1920s was the wealthiest town in the world. After Germany's defeat in World War One, South West Africa was handed over to South Africa who ruled it until independence in 1990. For a long time South Africa saw it as the fifth and wealthiest province in their country.

South Africa instituted some apartheid-inspired laws, moved coloureds and blacks into townships and gave the arable land to the whites.

Then in the late 1960s, black Namibians united under the banner of the South West Africa People's Organization (SWAPO) to fight for their independence. Over the next two decades they used guerrilla warfare against South African targets, infiltrating the territory from secret bases in Zambia and southern Angola.

Finally, South Africa conceded and agreed to hand over government to an independent Namibia in 1990. SWAPO leader Sam Nujoma, returned to Namibia after 30 years of exile and became president and administered a new constitution. Nujoma was succeeded in 2004 by Hifikepunye Pohamba, another founder of SWAPO. While continuing to be economically dependent on South Africa (especially for foodstuffs), Namibia is better off than many other countries in the region because of its diamond wealth.

1–5 Namibia is the ideal destination for overlanding. The wide open spaces cry out for exploration, and camping out under enormous starry skies is a real highlight.

THE OVERLAND ROUTE

From Zambia, Zimbabwe or the region around the Chobe National Park in Botswana, most overlanders enter Namibia via the Caprivi Strip, the narrow belt of greenery that hugs the Zambezi and Chobe rivers in the extreme northeast. It is a long narrow extension of land, running about 450 kilometres from the north-east corner of the main body of Namibia to the flood-plains and islands of the Zambezi River. The tarred Caprivi highway runs along its entire length and is in good condition. From Botswana's Okavango Delta, the alternative route is via Ghanzi in Botswana, to the east of Windhoek, the country's capital and a city steeped in German atmosphere.

From either direction, it's easy enough to explore the Etosha National Park in the northwest of the country, which warrants at least a couple of nights in the campsites which are close to floodlit waterholes that make for exciting night time game viewing. The park is very easy to get around in your own vehicle, and there are many opportunities to park at a waterhole to watch the animal action. Kaokoland, the harsh but scenic region around Opuwo to the north of Etosha, is home to the Himba people and life here hasn't changed much for hundreds of years. Travelling overland through this region you are likely to see the Himba carrying water or herding their cattle around their kraals. Just south of Etosha, there is the opportunity to meet cheetah at the Cheetah Park before travelling down the eerie Atlantic Coast. On the Skeleton Coast, so named for the shipwrecks that litter the shore, you can drive into Cape Cross, and from the car park see (and smell!) the breeding colony for seals.

Further south, Swakopmund, a quirky town situated between the desert and the ocean, is a delightful coastal oasis. It's a wonderful place to enjoy some unique adventure activities and lively evenings in the many good restaurants and bars, and most overlanders spend at least a couple of days here to make use of the town's facilities.

"the oldest desert on earth with the highest sand dunes in the world."

Continue south, and you will reach the Namib-Naukluft National Park, the oldest desert on earth with the highest sand dunes in the world. There are various nature walks in the area amongst the dunes and saltpans, and the scenic beauty of the shifting red-hued sand offers fantastic photography opportunities. The highlight here is to drive into the park at dawn and watch the sun rise over the sea of sand. Heading further south, you can visit the German folly, Duwisib Castle, and there is the option to travel to the coast again to Lüderitz, a small fishing port. Nearby is a town that was once of the world's wealthiest – Kolmanskop, an old diamond mining centre that is now a ghost town, its elaborate European houses now being encroached upon by the shifting desert.

Before reaching South Africa, the dramatic Fish River Canyon is just above the border, one of the natural wonders of Africa and at 500 metres deep and over 160 kilometres long, this is the second largest canyon in the world. You are able to drive your vehicle right to the lip for some outstanding views.

Caprivi Strip

The Caprivi Strip is the oddly-shaped panhandle that stretches between Angola and Botswana at the top of Namibia. It's enclosed by permanent water and starts at the Kavango River in the east, and follows the Zambezi River to the border junction of Namibia, Botswana, Zimbabwe and Zambia. You are bound to travel through it on any journey to or from these countries. Caprivi's main town, Katima Mulilo, is closer to Lusaka and Harare than it is to the Namibian capital. In many ways it's more like the countries that surround it than the rest of Namibia. Thanks to the rivers, the Caprivi is a lush tract of land, quite unlike the rest of the country's desert scenery. Game includes buffalo, elephant and healthy populations of hippo and crocodile. There are a number of campsites and lodges situated along the rivers that also offer access to the northern reaches of Botswana's Okavango Delta.

They are also only a short drive from Chobe National Park and Victoria Falls. The entire Western Caprivi today is a game reserve. There are over 8 000 elephant in this region as well as buffalo, hippo, and many antelope species. No permit is needed for using the Trans Caprivi Highway, but there are no fences, so keep your eyes open for animals when driving. In the western part of the Caprivi are the Popa Falls, which are a series of rapids where the Okavango River breaks through a four-metre-high rocky intrusion in its riverbed.

Windhoek

Thanks to a brilliant stroke of German planning, the capital city, Windhoek, is located slap bang in the middle of the country. With a population of around 200 000, it is an extremely small capital by global standards. Founded in 1840, it was often abandoned because of Nama-Herero wars. In 1890, the Germans reached there and established a fort. Today, the city centre is modern, extremely clean and is serviced by a well-developed infrastructure. It's a very un-African city characterised by German-style architecture – a lasting reminder of Namibia's early colonial history. Many streets are still named after Germans, and German is still one of the main languages spoken in Windhoek. It's a peaceful and relaxed city – so much so it verges on the slightly dull. It doesn't have too much to offer the visitor, but the shops sell pretty much anything you might like to buy, and there's a good European café culture. The city centre is small enough to explore on foot. Buildings of note include the Christuskirche (Christ Church) of the Lutheran parish from 1896, and the Alte Feste (Old Fort), the former headquarters of the Schutztruppe and today, Namibia's National Museum.

"It's a peaceful and relaxed city – so much so it verges on the slightly dull."

1 Sunset over the desert.
2 Namibia's attractive capital of Windhoek.

Etosha National Park

Etosha National Park is one of southern Africa's finest and most important game reserves covering an area of 22 270 square kilometres. It is home to 114 mammal species, 340 species of birds, and 110 reptilian species.

The park is dominated by the massive 5 000 square kilometre Etosha mineral pan – all that remains of an ancient lake. Etosha means 'Great White Place' in the Herero language and in the heat of the day the dried out surface of the pan is dazzlingly white. A lone wildebeest or herds of oryx can be seen crossing it or just standing, as if mesmerised.

In complete contrast, when the rain arrives, up to one metre of water turns the previously parched surface into an algae-rich lake that always attracts thousands of birds, including pink-tinged flamingos and pelicans.

Etosha has dozens of waterholes; some are natural while others are artificially fed from boreholes. These are ideal places to sit and wait for game, when a veritable Noah's Ark of species queue up to take a drink. The desert-dwelling oryx, upon which the mythical unicorn must surely be based, will certainly be seen, along with the impressive curly-horned kudu. Etosha also contains endangered black rhino and unusual species like the black-faced impala.

There are three rest camps in Etosha: Namutoni, Halali and Okaukuejo. Each has modern facilities including restaurants, shops and swimming pools with a perimeter fence making them safe to walk around. The highlight at the camps is the floodlit waterholes open for 24-hour game viewing. It's not uncommon to see a pride of lion or a family of rhino amble through the darkness. The game viewing is so good that people end up staying all night at the waterholes.

The best time to visit Etosha is in the cool dry winters when the animals stay closer to the waterholes.

1 Elephant at an Etosha waterhole.
2 Elephant from the driver's seat.
3 Lion on a salt pan.
4 Giraffe, zebra, springbok.
5 Female lion.

6 Oryx.
7 Etosha is said to have the tallest elephants in Africa, growing to measure up to four metres at the shoulder.
8 Warthogs.
9 Etosha Pan.
10 Zebra, springbok, elephant.

Cheetah Park

Just south of Etosha, and between Outjo and Kamanjab, is the Cheetah Park. Most overlanders stop here after leaving Etosha and the Cheetah Park has good facilities for campers and vehicles. There is the opportunity to get very close to some tame cheetah and the place to have your photograph taken next to one of Africa's most exotic animals. Namibia has more cheetah than anywhere else in Africa, but there is the ongoing problem of wild cheetah killing livestock on local farms. Shooting this wild cat is the practice amongst Namibian farmers, but the Cheetah Park gives the farmers an alternative by offering to trap any problem cheetah and relocate them to the Cheetah Park. Here they are released into a large and natural enclosure of 600 acres with other wild cats. At the park, visitors can meet tame cats, learn more about their behaviour, and watch the wild ones in the enclosure being fed.

1 The Cheetah Park offers excellent opportunities to get very close to cheetah and learn more about their behaviour. Having a photograph taken of you patting a cheetah is obligatory!

Damaraland

Damaraland is located to the north of Swakopmund and to the south of Etosha National Park. It's one of the most scenic regions of the country with a dramatic landscape of wide open sandy plains, massive granite koppies and red-hued mountains. It's also home to the elusive desert elephant and a few black rhino. Damaraland is derived from the Nama word '*Dama*', meaning 'who walked here'. It's the scenery and the anticipation of glimpsing an elephant's footprint that are the highlights of this region.

Twyfelfontein is home to the largest known concentration of Stone Age cave paintings in southern Africa, with approximately 2 500 engravings carved on a petrified sand dune. They date back to around 3 000 BC, and are easily accessible on foot accompanied by a guide. The best time to visit the area is in the late afternoon when the engravings catch the soft light just before sunset.

Twyfelfontein means 'doubtful spring' in Afrikaans, after a small natural spring in the area that produces only one cubic metre of water per day. When the site was named it was considered doubtful that one cubic metre of water could have supported man and animals for thousands of years. Evidently, from the existence of the rock paintings, it did.

Nearby is the Petrified Forest. This is not a frightened clump of trees but the site of some very old fossilised logs, thought to have been washed down an ancient river 250 million years ago. They became petrified, or fossilised, after being buried under tonnes of wet, silica-rich mud. There are around 50 trunks lying on the ground. The longest is 30 metres and you can still see the growth rings and bark on some of them.

2 A reliable 4x4 is necessary for exploring the dry riverbeds of this arid desert country.

3 One of the most dramatic rock formations in Namibia is the 35-metre-high pillar of limestone known as '*Vingerklip*' in Afrikaans, meaning the Rock Finger. It is an impressive lone relic of prehistoric erosion, and stands proudly above a valley roughly halfway between the Etosha National Park and Swakopmund in the heart of Damaraland.

4&5 Sightings of the hard-to-find desert elephant are one of the highlights of a trip to Damaraland.

6 Campsite near Sesfontein.

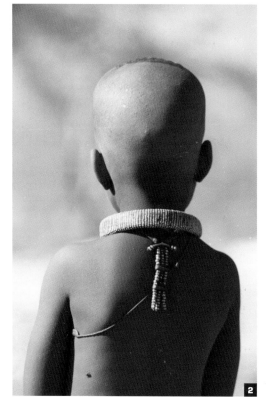

"One of the rarest of Africa's tribes, indisputably beautiful to photograph."

5

Himba

Namibia's Himba people are one of the rarest of Africa's tribes and indisputably one of the most beautiful to photograph. Increasingly being encroached upon by the modern world, only 6 000 of these self-sufficient nomadic people survive in the harsh but stunning corner of northwest Namibia known as Kaokoland. Their beehive huts are made from mopane tree saplings, covered with a mixture of mud and dung, and surrounded by a kraal where their animals are protected overnight against predators. Many settlements are often deserted as these pastoral people continuously wander with their herds in search of water and grazing, and visitors to the region may meet families on the move carrying all their worldly goods wrapped up in only animal skins.

The Himba are some of the most remarkable-looking people in Africa with their highly decorative and distinctive traditional dress. The women wear multi-layered skirts of goat skin and leather jewellery studded with shells and metal ore, as well as arm- and neckfuls of copper bangles. They are most renowned for the mixture with which they plaster their skin and hair: butter, ash, and red-hued ochre – a primitive protection against the sun which also keeps their skins looking younger. The result is quite dramatic. These women are literally painted red with incredibly smooth skin.

This Spread
1–5 Namibia's nomadic Himba are some of the most striking looking people in Africa, with their gleaming red skin, and elaborate hair and jewellery.

Rhino tracking

The desert-adapted black rhino inhabits the arid northwest of Namibia and is protected and monitored by the Save the Rhino Trust (SRT). Namibia is home to around a third of Africa's black rhino, and SRT has been instrumental in the recovery of what is Africa's last truly wild population. From Palmwag in Damaraland, there is the opportunity to go on a rhino track with the SRT staff and gain an amazing insight into the ecology and conservation of the region. It is usually possible to get extremely close to the rhino on foot.

Pages 230–231
A Himba mother leads her child across the desert.

This Page
1–3 Rhino tracking in Daramaland.

Cape Cross Seal Colony

Cape Cross is on the Skeleton Coast about 120 kilometres north of Swakopmund. It is the spot where Diego Cão, a Portuguese sailor, set foot on what is now Namibia in 1486. He was the first European to arrive on the Atlantic coast and he erected a cross here as a navigational aid. Today, Cape Cross is a popular tourist attraction, not because of its stone cross, but because of its seal colony. Exactly why the seals congregate here is not known, but congregate they do. At certain times of the year as many as 80 000 seals choose to sit on the same rocky area or frolic in the surrounding waves and surf.

The rutting season is around October to November and each bull seal has about 5-25 cows in his harem. He fiercely defends his females and much fighting goes on amongst the bulls as the cows give birth. Fully grown bulls can weigh up to 360 kilograms. They lose a lot of their fat in the first six weeks of breeding season whilst actively defending their territory. Between December and February, the females give birth; each female has one pup, and only seven days after giving birth, the rutting season begins again. Pups have black fur and have a very strong relationship with their mothers. Unfortunately Cape Cross is so crowded with seals that many pups get crushed to death or taken by predators. About 25 percent of the pups die during this time, and seeing Cape Cross then is not for the squeamish. Otherwise it's a wildlife spectacle not to be missed.

The presence of so many seals also attracts other wildlife. Predators such as black-backed jackal and brown hyena are often seen on the Skeleton Coast. They are drawn to this otherwise barren region by the abundance of easy food in the form of seal pups. Seals consume a lot of fish – up to 8 percent of their own body weight daily. As you can imagine, with all those seals eating all those fish, Cape Cross qualifies as The Smelliest Place on Earth!

1–4 Cape Cross Seal Colony on the Skeleton Coast; thousands of seals congregate on a rocky peninsula that was visited by the Portuguese in the 15th century.

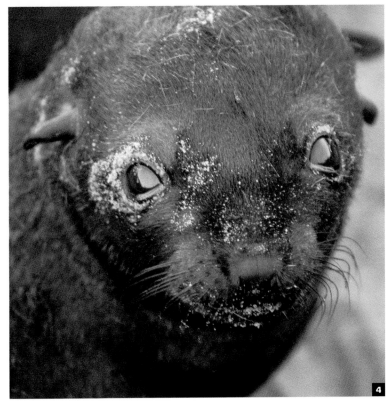

1 Cape Cross Seal Colony soon after the birthing season. Baby seals have black fur. Note the solitary penguin in this picture.

Spitzkoppe

The Spitzkoppe between Usakos and Swakopmund is by no means Namibia's highest mountain, but due to its striking outline, it is regarded as the most well-known mountain in the country. The dramatic rock formation of Spitzkoppe was formed by subterranean volcanic activity years ago and was slowly exposed as the surrounding ground eroded. It is an inselberg, which means island mountain, and it stands out isolated in the surrounding plains. Spitzkoppe is well worth visiting just to drink in the incredible scenery and is a great place for camping amongst the acacia trees filled with the delicate nests of masked weaver birds. At sunset, the rocks are the colour of sienna, rust, and ochre.

1–3 Camping amongst the boulders of Spitzkoppe. There are fine views from the rocks, especially at sunset.

Swakopmund

All travellers to Namibia will end up at the coastal town of Swakopmund. Once a sleepy town of Bavarian beer maidens and German patisseries, Swakopmund is fast becoming the adrenalin capital of Namibia. It lies at the tail end of the infamous Skeleton Coast, which today lures optimistic anglers and crayfish divers rather than the doomed shipwrecked sailors after which it was named. For a seaside resort, Swakopmund borders on the bizarre. Pounded by the harsh Atlantic Ocean, the strip of foggy coastline supports windswept dunes and desolate gravel plains. But when the sun is out, the brightly painted buildings shine gaily, the ocean sparkles and the town is bathed in a friendly and relaxed holiday atmosphere.

Swakopmund straddles the dusty Swakop riverbed. The Swakop is dry most of the time except when there's excessive flooding. This is a rare occurrence, as it hardly ever rains. The coast road south, where shifting dunes are regularly pushed off the tarmac by bulldozers, leads to neighbouring Walvis Bay.

To the north are the fishing town of Henties Bay and Cape Cross Seal Colony. Further north, the road passes through gradual desolation until it gets to the forbidding and eerie Skeleton Coast National Park. Sand surrounds Swakopmund in every direction, and the sea of dunes beginning at the back of the town leads south towards the mighty Namib-Naukluft Park.

German settlers arrived on the bleak coast in 1892. The first building erected was a garrison and barracks for soldiers and sailors. The settlement grew quickly using materials imported from Germany (there was, after all, not a tree in sight). An iron jetty, that still stands today, was constructed to receive ships laden with imports for what was then the German Protectorate of Deutsche Südwestafrika. German traders set up their offices and businesses here. But when South Africa took control in 1915, the ships and trade moved to the deeper harbour at Walvis Bay and Swakopmund sank into economic decline. With the discovery of uranium at Rossing 40 kilometres away, the town was revitalised. The potential of Swakopmund as an attractive seaside resort (unlike industrial Walvis Bay) for travel-restricted South Africans during apartheid was realised. It has grown considerably since Namibia gained independence in 1990, and is still growing today. Much of the local economy relies on tourism, and

4&5 Swakopmund's architecture lends itself to German colonial influence. There are a number of old buildings from that era and also many new buildings have been built in the same style.

there is a staggering array of activities and beautiful landscapes in the surrounding area.

The town has an undoubtedly German feel about it – half-timbered houses, pretty gardens and colonial architecture. It's easy to forget you are actually in Africa, especially in the many coffee and cake shops or pubs and taverns. You won't have a problem finding an apple strudel or a flagon of beer in this town. Swakopmund provides a welcome urban release from Namibia's open spaces. Suddenly you'll find shops, bars, movie theatres and all those other convenient services that you may have craved out in the bush. It's worthwhile taking a stroll around town and the brightly-painted buildings are very photogenic on a sunny afternoon. These include the elaborate old train station, built in 1901, that has now been converted into the Swakopmund Hotel and Casino; the impressive Hohenzollern building, built in 1906 as Swakopmund's first hotel; and the prominent Damara Tower, which once served as a water tower and a landmark for traders arriving by ox wagons from the interior. Anyone partial to the golden nectar should head for the Hansa Brewery, the source of Namibia's most popular beer. The National Marine Aquarium showcases what lies beneath the nearby

Atlantic Ocean in a number of roomy aquariums. The largest has a unique tunnel to walk through where you can eye a giant manta ray or look directly into the mouth of a shark. The Swakopmund Museum, at the foot of another of the town's famous landmarks – the red-and-white-striped lighthouse – has some excellent exhibits explaining what goes on at Rossing Uranium Mine, 55 kilometres east of Swakopmund. There are also interesting mock-ups of house interiors giving a feel of how the early German settlers lived, as well as some informative sections on Namibia's flora and fauna.

Just outside Swakopmund across the Swakop riverbed, a section of towering dunes has been set aside for activities including sand boarding and quad biking. Water-based activities include boat trips to see dolphins and seals, shore-based angling (some of the best in Africa), deep-sea fishing, crayfish diving, surfing or simply lazing on the beach. Remember though, this is the Atlantic, and whilst you can swim safely from Swakopmund's beach, the water is often freezing. Swakopmund is on the edge of the Namib Desert. This is best appreciated from the air on a scenic flight, or alternatively, you can jump out of a plane from 12 000 feet on a tandem parachute jump.

Sky-diving

With clear skies and a starkly beautiful coastline, Swakopmund is the perfect destination to go sky-diving – Namibia's ultimate adrenalin activity. The Swakopmund Skydiving Club offers extremely popular tandem free-fall jumps for novices. Jumps take place daily, normally after the fog has lifted in the morning. After a brief safety chat, you board a small plane for a 35-minute scenic flight over Swakopmund and the surrounding coast and desert as you prepare yourself for your jump. This involves being strapped between the thighs of your tandem jump master and shuffling to the door of the plane. At 12 000 feet you both tumble into the sky for a mind-blowing 30 second free-fall at around 220 kilometres per hour – a totally exhilarating experience. Then the parachute opens and you float to the ground for a 10-minute ride enjoying the breathtaking desert scenery.

Scenic flights

Namibia is really a country that is best appreciated from the air, and sightseeing flights are a great way to admire the unusual and dramatic landscapes. On offer from Swakopmund and Walvis Bay into most parts of Namibia, flights vary from one-and-a-half hour flips along the coast to all-day safaris to northern Namibia that include landings and 4x4 adventures. From the air you can clearly see Namibia's desert landscapes, dried-up riverbeds, moonscapes, rock formations, mountains and gravel plains. Along the

1 The restored Otavi-Bahn railway station.
2–5 Sky-diving over Swakopmund.

coast you can fly over thousands of flamingos and pelicans on the lagoons south of Walvis Bay, or seals and dolphins to the north of Swakopmund at Cape Cross. Flights that follow the infamous and treacherous Skeleton Coast offer views of the harsh coastline and gloomy shipwrecks pounded by the Atlantic Ocean.

Inland, the seemingly endless sand dunes are a spectacular sight. You can fly right over Sossusvlei before heading back to Swakopmund over Namibia's Diamond Restricted Area and the remains of abandoned diamond camps. To the north, flights go past Namibia's highest mountain, the Brandberg, over Damaraland and Kaokoland to Opuwo. In Opuwo, there's the opportunity to land and visit an authentic Himba village.

Fishing

The Namibian coast, known for its unique scenic beauty, is also regarded as one of the best fishing grounds in the world. Fishing is good from Sandwich Harbour, south of Walvis Bay, up to Terrace Bay in the Skeleton Coast National Park. Fishing trips can be done either by boat or from the shore and no previous experience is required. This is a great place to try fishing if you've never done it before.

Full-day, all-inclusive trips are on offer and fishermen are allowed to keep their catch to cook and eat that night, though shark fishing follows a tag-and-release policy and crayfish may only be caught in season. Deep-sea game fishing for snoek, yellowtail and tuna is done in ski boats which are fully equipped with all the necessary angling equipment, bait, fish-finder equipment and experienced guides.

On the shore, surf angling on Namibia's Atlantic coast is regarded as some of the best in Africa. Thousands of anglers from all over southern Africa visit Swakopmund and Henties Bay each year. The best time for angling is between November and March.

Sand-boarding

Namibia is famous for its giant sand dunes, and there's no better way to conquer these than to zoom down them head first on a traditional Swakopmund sand-board, or carve up the dune with style and skill on a snowboard adapted for sand. The beauty about sand-boarding is the sand is not abrasive, and as it's obviously not cold, you can board in shorts and t-shirts. The worst that can happen is that you walk away covered in sand. For the lie-down option you're supplied with a large flat piece of waxed hardboard, safety hat, elbow guards and gloves before heading off to climb a dune. The idea is to lie on the board, push off from the top and speed head first down the slippery surface. Speeds easily reach 80 kilometres per hour and some of the dunes are very steep, though first you'll do a few training rides on the lower dunes.

Stand-up boarding requires more skill. It is exactly the same as snowboarding, but on sand, using standard snowboarding equipment to surf your way down the dunes.

Sand-boarding is also an environmentally friendly activity. The dunes are constantly shifting and can move at the astonishing rate of ten metres in a week; sand-board tracks soon disappear.

Quad-biking

Another way to explore the dune field near Swakopmund is by quad-bike – a 4-wheel, all-terrain motorbike. This is one of the best ways to access parts of the Swakopmund sand dunes that even 4x4 cars can't reach. No previous motor biking experience is needed, and there are two types of bike to choose from. For those who are a little unsure of their biking prowess, there are 160cc semi-automatic bikes. Those who wish to go hell for leather and have some idea of what they are doing can ride the 200cc manual quad-bikes. Helmets, goggles and gloves are provided, and tours are multi-guiding with slow and fast groups.

1–5 Sand-boarding on the dunes around Swakopmund. There are two options; lie-down or stand-up. Who would have thought sand could be so interesting?

"The dunes are constantly shifting and can move at the astonishing rate of ten metres in a week... tracks soon disappear."

1–6 Quad-biking through the sand dunes around Swakopmund is lots of fun and anyone can have a go. The ride varies from fast dashes across stony desert, to sweeping curves through soft sand up the side of a dune.

7&8 The Welwitschia is an unusual and ancient plant that only grows on the gravel plains of the Namib and relies on the coastal fogs for water. The oldest living specimen has been dated at 2 000 years old.

9 When travelling by road, ensure you have adequate drinking water as there are some long distances between places and it gets very hot in the desert.

Namib-Naukluft Park

The Namib Desert is between 80 and 250 kilometres wide and stretches along Namibia's coastline from the Orange River in the south to just north of the Kunene River. It's the oldest desert on Earth and home to some truly bizarre life forms – animals, insects and plants that have adapted to this inhospitable region by surviving on the life-giving moisture from the sea mists that roll for 100 kilometres inland. Much of the Namib Desert is situated within the 50 000 square kilometre Namib-Naukluft Park, one of the largest national parks in Africa. In the Nama language, Namib means vast. The Namib is most famous for its towering rust-red sand dunes, blown into razor sharp ridges and peaks by the wind. The 300-metre dunes at Sossusvlei, in the heart of the desert, are the tallest in the world.

Sossusvlei is surely one of the most spectacular sights in Africa. The best time to visit is at sunrise, when the play of light and shadow gives the desert landscape tints and textures. Colours are strong and constantly changing, allowing for wonderful photographic opportunities. Climbing one of the dunes provides awesome views of the sea of sand and a sense of complete timelessness and solitude.

The campsite at Sesriem is the closest accommodation to Sossusvlei and the only place from where you are allowed to drive out for sunrise in the dunes. It's a stunning desert spot to camp under a huge night-time sky. Sossusvlei is around 60 kilometres or one hour's drive from Sesriem, and to cover the last four kilometres to Sossusvlei, you'll need to use a 4x4 vehicle or walk. Walking is best as there is no better way to experience the silence of the vast and eerie dunes. For an aerial perspective, there is the option of taking a scenic flight from Swakopmund or a hot-air balloon from Sesriem for the best view you will ever get of an endless, rippling desert.

1–12 The dunes around Sossusvlei cry out for exploration, and climbing a giant sand dune is a Namibia 'must-do'. The best time to visit is either at sunrise or sunset when the changing hues of orange and gold deepen with the sun. It hardly ever rains here and the earth is parched and cracked, whilst the few hardy trees struggle to survive in the treacherous heat.

"It's the oldest desert on Earth and home to some truly bizarre life forms."

"Sossusvlei is surely one of the most spectacular sights in Africa
– constantly changing, allowing for photographic opportunities."

1 Sossusvlei, Namib-Naukluft Park.
2 Climbing a giant sand dune.
3 Driving through the desert.
4 Campsite at the Namib-Naukluft Park.

Ballooning

Ballooning over the Namib Desert is a captivating way to view the immense and extraordinary panorama of the contoured dunes and stark desert plains, as the rising sun paints the sand in warm red light. Flights begin near Sesriem, and because of the strong thermal movements over the desert, the balloon takes off at dawn. Here you can enjoy a spectacular sunrise over the world's oldest desert and soar with the winds over an ocean of sand and mountains. Balloon rides last for one hour and are followed by a celebratory champagne breakfast at a landing spot in the middle of nowhere.

Desert walking

Guided walks can be taken in the sand dunes around Sossusvlei. This is the best way to learn about the desert environment and guides point out the tracks in the sand of small animals and insects, and explain how the larger animals of the Namib, such as oryx, survive in the seemingly waterless environment.

Duwisib Castle

Duwisib Castle, to the east of the Namib-Naukluft Park, is an impressive fortress of stone as luxurious as a European stately home, and a folly for its extraordinary desert location. Completed in 1909 for a young and eccentric German army captain, Baron Hans-Heinrich von Wolf and his American-born wife Jayta, it is in the style of an authentic German fort. The architect, Wilhelm Sander, also built other forts in Namibia at Namutoni (now a rest camp in the Etosha National Park) and Windhoek.

The newlyweds arrived from Germany and decided to settle in what was then South West Africa and bought farmland covering over 1 400 square kilometres. The Baron desired a grand house on his property, and as he was a military man, one that was extremely secure. The result

1 Ballooning over the Namib Desert.
2 Guided walks to learn more about the unsual flora and fauna of the desert.
3 Feral horses on the road to Lüderitz.
4 A road sign stating the obvious.

was a sandstone fortress with high walls and turrets, which enclosed a 22-roomed palace full of nineteenth century antiques, exquisite paintings and a collection of rifles and swords. Stone came from a local quarry, but all the other materials and fittings were imported from Germany, and transported 640 kilometres across the unforgiving Namib Desert by ox wagon from the ports of Lüderitz and Swakopmund. The rooms line a shady courtyard of lawns and jacaranda trees, and once inside the cool walls surrounded by delicate furniture and fine artwork, it's easy to forget you are in the middle of Namibia's wilderness.

Lüderitz & Kolmanskop

Lüderitz is a quirky little town centred around what is one of the best harbours on the inhospitable coast of Namibia. The only road in and out of Lüderitz crosses the desert from Keetmanshoop further inland. Along this road are signs warning of 'Sand' and 'Wind', and the closer to the coast you get, the more sandy and windy it gets. Also on the approach to Lüderitz you may encounter an unlikely desert dweller – there is a herd of feral horses that lives in this region of hot, gravel-strewn plains. Their hardiness in the face of extremely harsh climatic conditions is extraordinary. Just off the Lüderitz road is a lookout point above a water trough where the horses gather to drink. It is not known how long they have lived in this region, though it is generally believed that they have been here since German times. One theory is that the horses are descendents from thoroughbreds that were being sent by ship from Europe to Australia. The ship ran aground near the mouth of the Orange River, and it is possible that the strongest horses could have reached the shore.

Lüderitz itself was founded by the Germans in 1883, as a trading post and fishing harbour. When diamonds were discovered in the region in 1909, it enjoyed some prosperity, though little

has changed here since then. Lüderitz does however suffer from a severe climate and the wind that comes in from the Atlantic Ocean is not only strong but icy cold too. There are frequent sea fogs and sand storms – after driving in from the blistering desert, the temperature drops sharply at the coast. There are some scenic old buildings cluttered around the small but colourful harbour. The most striking are Goerke-Haus, a former magistrate's residence built in 1909, and the Lutheran Church on the hill above the bay, known as the Felsenkirche, which was built in 1912. A monument of Adolf Lüderitz, the German founder of the town, stands on Shark Island, from where there are excellent views of the town. Possibly one of the windiest campsites in the world is also located on Shark Island.

At Diaz Point, south of Lüderitz, there is a stone cross commemorating Bartholomew Diaz's discovery of the area in 1487. There is also a Floating Diamond Museum on an old diamond boat with exhibitions on diamond diving and oyster fishing. The Lüderitz area is home to a large number of flamingos, cormorants and seagulls which inhabit the shallow lagoons, and boat trips from the harbour visit colonies of seals and penguins which live on the coast rocky islands.

One of Lüderitz's main attractions is Kolmanskop Ghost Town perched on an exposed dune off the approach road to town. It endures battering weather conditions, including gale force winds capable of moving acres of sand. Abandoned in the 1950s, it was once the centre of one of Africa's leading economic phenomena – the discovery of diamonds. For a short period at the beginning of the century, Kolmanskop was the centre of the West Coast diamond rush which brought prospectors from the German colony's homeland in droves. The first Namibian diamond was found in 1908, and even today, the combined output of South Africa, Namibia, and Botswana produces the greatest volume and value of diamonds on the globe.

The town of Kolmanskop rapidly emerged from the desert, and it was said that diamonds were so common, they could be plucked from the sand by moonlight. Over half a century, 25 million carats were extracted from the sand. Kolmanskop boomed, and luxurious houses and administrative centres were constructed, along with a bakery, butchery, general dealer, lemonade and ice fac-

"Diamonds were so common, they could be plucked from the sand by moonlight"

1 The view from the top of Fish River Canyon.
2 The second largest canyon in the world, the Fish River winds through the canyon 500 metres below.
3 Deserted house at Kolmanskop ghost town.
4 Quiver tree.
5 The viewpoint at the top of Fish River Canyon is the perfect place to watch the sunset.

Pages 252–253
Overland truck at the top of Fish River Canyon.

tory, school, and a fully equipped hospital which boasted the first X-ray machine in Africa and its own wine cellar. During the 1920s it was the wealthiest town on Earth, and European lifestyles had been recreated in an African wilderness.

The diamonds eventually ran out, and the last family departed Kolmanskop in 1956 and left it to the desert and the ghosts. No one was there to stop the pace of the ever-shifting dunes as they eased their way slowly up against walls, and seeped through doorways and windowsills, filling the innards of beautifully constructed buildings. Today some of these have been restored and house a museum of abandoned items, but the majority of the buildings have been left as they were.

Fish River Canyon

The Fish River Canyon is situated in the far south of Namibia, close to the border with South Africa. The ravine winds over a distance of 160 kilometres, is 500 metres deep in places and 27 kilometres across at its widest point.

It's the largest canyon in Africa and second biggest in the world. Only the Grand Canyon in the USA tops it. The 650-kilometre Fish River is Namibia's longest. It rises in the eastern Naukluft Mountains and flows southwest through the canyon into the Orange River. The river meanders so widely that a straight line distance of 32 kilometres is more than doubled by the river's course on the canyon floor. In the winter, during the dry season, there is little water and at the driest times, often only small stagnant pools remain. Summer rains transform it into a rapid river.

The Fish River Canyon is thought to have been created over 500 million years ago by water erosion and movements in the earth's crust. There are several viewpoints along the western rim with splendid views of the dramatic canyon: a perfect position for watching a spectacular desert sunset when the steep cliffs are awash with colour. From the main viewpoint there's a path of sorts to the bottom of the canyon. This is a popular hike at sunrise before it gets too hot. Be warned though: you need to be fit as it's a rocky and strenuous climb. Temperatures in the summer can reach some 50 degrees Celsius and the canyon is closed to hikers at this time.

The campsite at the top of the canyon is called Hobas, located ten kilometres from the viewpoints at the canyon rim. The resort at the end and bottom of the canyon is Ai-Ais, meaning 'burning water' in the Nama language. This refers to the hot springs that have been channelled into various indoor and outdoor swimming pools. Between November and February, Ai-Ais is also closed. When temperatures in the shade are well over 50 degrees Celsius, the last thing anyone wants to do is splash around in a hot spring!

SOUTH AFRICA

South Africa is one of the most beautiful and varied countries in the world with a constantly sunny climate and a wonderful range of landscapes, and as such has much more to offer than is possible to see in one trip. It is located, as one might expect, on the southern tip of Africa, and with over 4 000 kilometres of coastline, its shores are swept by the cool Atlantic currents around the Cape, while the warm Indian Ocean gives rise to a tropical feel in the east. Along its northern border, from west to east, lie Namibia, Botswana and Zimbabwe. To the northeast are Mozambique and Swaziland. Wholly enclosed by South Africa is the independent kingdom of Lesotho on the eastern side of the country.

South Africa's main attraction is its magnificent natural beauty, represented in a multitude of game reserves and national parks. The other major draw is its vibrant cities, such as Cape Town, Johannesburg and Durban, full of the cosmopolitan populations you'd expect from the 'Rainbow Nation'. Outdoor activity is very much a part of life, be it hiking and surfing, or one of the booming adrenalin sports. Its history too is fascinating, with numerous historical towns, townships and battle sites worth visiting. In short, the choice of destinations, activities and itineraries is virtually inexhaustible, so careful planning is needed to make the best use of your time. The tourist board calls it 'a world in one country' – corny but true. The climatic, cultural and geographical differences make it a playground for the adventurous traveller. Driving is easy; campsites and accommodation plentiful, and even the remotest areas are accessible. The road network is excellent and routes are well signposted, making travel a hassle-free experience. The only problem is that there's so much to fit in!

The Northern Cape Province is a semi-desert area which stretches from the Karoo in the south to the Kalahari in the north. The main city is Kimberley, famous for the largest diamond rush in history, which took place from 1871. The Big Hole remains as a monument to these hard and hopeful days. In the north of the province lie the Richtersveld National Park and the region of Namaqualand. The landscape is stark and rugged and the climate is hot and dry, but when the seasonal rains come in spring, the area is miraculously transformed into a carpet of colourful flowers. In the extreme north is the Kgalagadi Transfrontier Park which shares an unfenced border with Botswana to allow free movement of the many migratory animals. On the Namibia border, the Orange River plummets over the Augrabies Falls, where plentiful wildlife thrives along its banks.

The Western Cape Province is one of the country's most geographically diverse. Cape Town is the oldest city in South Africa, and with Table Mountain as a dramatic backdrop, it is one of the most beautiful cities in the world. Highlights here are the busy harbour, the fishing villages around the Cape Peninsula, innumerable beaches along its two shorelines, several nature reserves including the Cape of Good Hope Reserve, Kirstenbosch National Botanical Garden, and the Waterfront complex. In Cape Town you can also catch a glimpse of South Africa's brittle past on a visit to Robben Island, where Nelson Mandela was held in prison, or to a township. The Cape Winelands provide a beautiful setting to sample the best of South African wines, with quaint cottages, manicured rolling wine estates and misty mountains. The Garden Route is the stretch of land and coastline that runs between Mossel Bay and Storms River, where there are lakes, mountains, golden beaches, cliffs and dense indigenous forests. The towns offer good accommodation options, shopping and eating.

From the Tsitsikamma National Park in the south to Port Edward in the north, the Eastern Cape Province features 800 kilometres of pristine natural and cultural attractions. The former

"The tourist board calls it 'a world in one country' – corny but true. The contrasts make it a playground for the adventurous traveller."

Transkei region is known as the Wild Coast. Stormy and windswept, this is where many famous shipwrecks have occurred. It is also a place of picturesque and untouched shorelines featuring swathes of empty beaches and rural Xhosa villages. The Addo Elephant National Park is an essential stop to see elephants as well as numerous other species of game. Jeffreys Bay is one of the world's great surfing sites with a chilled-out holiday atmosphere where surfers pit themselves against the rolling waves.

On South Africa's east coast is the province of KwaZulu-Natal, one of the greenest and best-watered areas of the country. It is bordered by the dramatic uKhahlamba Drakensberg National Park, a World Heritage Site, which has several peaks well over 3 000 metres, rugged green hills and deep-cut valleys. Along the KwaZulu-Natal coast, golden brown beaches are a magnet to the traveller seeking sun and a sub-tropical climate. Durban is a holiday city with gleaming seafront hotels and miles of beaches edging the Indian Ocean. South Africa's biggest harbour is situated in Durban which is the busiest port in sub-Saharan Africa. In the interior of the province are the extensive battlefield sites from the Boer and Zulu wars of the nineteenth century. On the northern coastline is the Greater St Lucia Wetland Park, another World Heritage Site, with vast lagoons full of hippos and crocodiles. Elsewhere in the province are several parks including Ithala, Mkuze, and Hluhluwe-Imfolozi, the latter being an important sanctuary for black and white rhino.

Bordering Mozambique in the east, Mpumalanga is well known for its spectacular scenery, wildlife and historical interest. The highveld above Kruger supports waterfalls and pretty country towns and the dramatic Blyde River Canyon, the third largest in the world. Pilgrim's Rest is a historic gold rush town where the original miners' cottages have been restored as museums, craft shops and restaurants. The first national park created in Africa, the Greater Kruger National

Park covers an area of over 24 000 square kilometres of game-rich bush. The park's rest camps provide good facilities and a little luxury can be combined with game viewing at the many private lodges on the western edge of Kruger.

To the north of the country, Johannesburg is the commercial and business centre of South Africa. The city was established when gold was discovered in 1886, and since then it has grown from a shanty town to a modern sophisticated city. Adjoining the city is Soweto, the largest black residential area in South Africa, where you can learn the story of South Africa on a township tour. Most of the world's leading airlines fly into Johannesburg International Airport, which is one of the busiest airports in the Southern Hemisphere. Pretoria to the north of Johannesburg is South Africa's administrative capital. Founded in the nineteenth century by the Voortrekkers, it is often referred to as the 'jacaranda city', after the thousands of trees lining the streets with their purple blossoms.

In the Free State is the scenic highland area of the Golden Gate National Park, with its striking sandstone rock formations, and towns such as Clarens where there are a number of art galleries and traditional craft centres. The North-West Province is an agricultural region but is home to the casino and resort of Sun City, and the adjacent Pilanesberg National Park. Not far to the north lies the Madikwe Game Reserve where a project to restock the wildlife has ensured that there are plentiful game-viewing opportunities, especially of the endangered wild dog. The Limpopo Province occupies ten percent of South Africa and shares the Limpopo River with its northern neighbour Zimbabwe. Here is the northern part of the Greater Kruger National Park, and the N1, part of the Great North Road that heads north into Zimbabwe and effectively links South Africa with the rest of the continent.

There is enough in South Africa to keep adventurers occupied for months. The beautiful city of Cape Town is a hive of activity, the most

obvious one being climbing or riding the cable car to the top of Table Mountain. The Cape beaches offer horse trails and surfing, or you can slip down the dunes on a sand board. In the Cape canyons you can try kloofing – a combination of trekking, climbing and sliding down waterfalls. Along the coast you can watch whales, paddle with the jackass penguins, witness the sardine run and go cage-diving with a great white shark. Along the Garden Route, you can explore caves, ride ostriches and eat oysters and bungee off the Bloukrans Bridge – the highest bungee jump in the world. The five-day Otter Trail hike runs through the fabulous Tsitsikamma National Park, where gorges are run by wild black-water tube rides. The Drakensberg Mountains are hiker's heaven or you can go horse-riding in the foothills on the Lesotho border. Sodwana National Park is a fantastic place to learn to dive and the wetlands and beaches of St Lucia are a hotspot for angling, game fishing and snorkelling. Jeffreys Bay is home to South Africa's premier surfing scene.

SOUTH AFRICA'S HISTORY

Evidence of human occupation of South Africa extends back 40 000 years, when the Khoi Khoi and San peoples occupied the land. Later they were joined by the Bantu who migrated from the north. The Europeans landed at Table Bay from the seventeenth century. The Dutch (Boers) staked out the land and began their Great Trek to the interior, where they established the new colonies of the Orange Free State and the Transvaal. The British controlled the towns and coast. A century of skirmish, conflict and casualty ensued between the British, the Boers and the tribes who owned the land that they desired so much.

The discovery of diamonds, and later gold in the Transvaal at the end of the nineteenth century, resulted in an English invasion which sparked the second Anglo-Boer War. Lives were lost on a massive scale before British victory in 1902. The Union of South Africa was established to

mend the country they had nearly destroyed. An uneasy power-sharing between the two groups held sway until the 1940s, when the Afrikaner National Party was able to gain a strong majority. This had disastrous consequences for the black people of South Africa. Increasingly repressive legislation was introduced and apartheid ('being apart') reared its ugly head. Pass laws and classification forced blacks to live separate and inferior lives. Race laws touched every aspect of social life, including a prohibition of marriage between non-whites and whites, and the sanctioning of 'white-only' jobs, services and public places. Non-compliance was dealt with harshly. All blacks were required to carry pass books. In 1960 black demonstrators in Sharpeville who refused to carry their pass books clashed with the police. The conflict left 69 people dead, and the government declared a state of emergency. Homelands were created from 1976 to 1981 as independent states ensuring the preservation of white supremacy elsewhere. The homelands denationalised nine million black South Africans who now needed passports to enter South Africa: they were aliens in their own country.

The principal black opposition movement was the African National Congress (ANC). The bulk of the ANC's organisation including its military wing worked in exile. During the state of emergency which continued intermittently until 1989, thousands of activists of the ANC and other groups were arrested. Some died in police custody and others were either banished from the country or imprisoned for life. Nelson Mandela was one of these.

In the 1989 elections, the hard-line national party president, PW Botha, gave way to the much more progressive FW De Klerk. The new government faced constant pressure from the international community and human rights bodies to dismantle apartheid. Over the next 12 months, the De Klerk government removed the ban on the ANC, the South African Communist Party and 30 other anti-apartheid groups. They released the jailed ANC leadership including its leader Nelson Mandela, who had been imprisoned for 27 years. Mandela and his ANC colleagues immediately started negotiating a political settlement with the white government. After years of struggle during one of the most politically turbulent periods on Earth, the ANC was democratically elected to power in 1994. Mandela as president created the 'Rainbow Nation'. De Klerk became deputy president and he and Mandela jointly won the Nobel Peace Prize. The priorities for the new government were straightforward but daunting: to provide decent standards of housing, education, and health care to the majority black population – needs that had been ignored under the apartheid regime. Before the 1999 elections, Mandela announced that he would not stand for a second term and passed the presidential reins to Thabo Mbeki. Mandela is still one of Africa's finest statesmen and the majority of South Africans hold great respect and admiration for him. The depth of change required in South Africa is enormous – poverty, unemployment and crime are problems that will take generations to overcome – but an atmosphere of freedom and hope has settled over the new South Africa.

THE OVERLAND ROUTE

South African roads are probably the best there are in Africa, though road accident statistics are high and caution is required when driving. Most overland tours between Kenya and the Cape naturally finish or start in Cape Town. From the north, it only takes a couple of days to drive from the Namibian border to Cape Town, with perhaps a couple of overnight stops en route at either the Orange River on the border where there are campsites and the opportunity to canoe on the river, or at the wine estates around Stellenbosch and Paarl. Then on the last day of the tour, trucks make the final drive towards Table Mountain. Most groups enjoy a big night out in Cape Town to celebrate

the end of their tour. The city warrants at least a few days to explore and there are a number of things to see and do. It's also good to rest up, get used to not being in the truck, sleep in a proper bed, and work out how to fit all the souvenirs you have bought on the tour into your backpack. From Cape Town some travellers return directly home, while others continue to explore South Africa. Some overland companies offer short overland tours between Cape Town and Johannesburg, or alternatively many overlanders will hire a car with some of the new friends they made on the trip. There are also buses including the hop-on, hop-off Baz Bus which is ideal for backpackers, and South Africa does not present any problems to explore independently.

For many independent overlanders, Cape Town is the very end of their trip, and for those who have crossed much of the continent, there is a great sense of achievement to gaze upon Table Mountain after months and months of driving through Africa. It is traditional to drive all the way to the end of the Cape Peninsula and have a celebratory photograph taken at the Cape of Good Hope and Cape Point, or even as far as Cape Agulhas, the southernmost point of Africa where the Indian and Atlantic oceans meet. These travellers may go on to drive around South Africa, but to reach Cape Town epitomises the end of the trip – the completion of an epic and unforgettable physical and mental journey.

For those travelling north, it is the beginning, where the anticipation of what lies ahead in Africa has only just been born.

"The completion of an epic and unforgettable physical and mental journey from the top of Africa to the bottom."

Pages 258–259
For most overlanders travelling through Africa, Cape Town is either the end or the start of the journey.

This Spread
1 Table Mountain National Park is world famous for its diverse variety of plant species.

Northern Cape Province

Arriving from Namibia, the first province of South Africa is the Northern Cape Province which is a largely empty region. It is dominated by the immense and spacious plains of the Great Karoo, covered with grass and acacia trees, and some hardy and far-flung villages and farms. The wide-open spaces are characterized by clear crisp skies, flamboyant sunsets, brilliant starry nights and enormous sheep farms. To serve the needs of the farmers, there are a few typical South African dorps (Afrikaans for village), each dominated by an imposing Dutch Reformed Church. On the wild and lonely West Coast the remote fishing communities and bird colonies lead on to flower-rich Namaqualand. In spring the grassy plains explode with colour from millions of wild flowers. In the far north, the landscape reaches to the quiver tree-spotted deserts of southern Namibia. Here the vast expanses of arid and spacious semi-desert known as the Richtersveld are blazed by the hot sun in summer and frozen at night in the winter. The green agricultural belt, which flanks the Orange River as it nears the Atlantic Ocean, provides a lush contrast to the ruggedness of the Richtersveld. Most overlanders stop at the campsites along the river and it's a great spot for a canoe ride between Namibia and South Africa. Local operators offer gentle floats downstream and it is a relaxing way to spend a morning or afternoon. The unique experience here is paddling along in no-man's land between the two countries.

1 Flamboyant sunsets
 characterise the
 Northern Cape.
2 Canoeing on the
 Orange River.
3 The Orange River marks the
 border between South Africa
 and Namibia.
4 Namaqualand in the
 Northern Cape Province is
 ablaze with colour during the
 flower season.

Pages 264–265
Southern Right whale
showing off in the waves.

"The vast expanses of arid and spacious semi-desert are blazed by
the hot sun in summer and frozen at night in the winter."

Western Cape

Overlanders heading for Cape Town from Namibia will pass through the Western Cape, arguably South Africa's most diverse landscape. The Cape West Coast is dry, rugged and dotted with small fishing villages. Inland the Cedarberg mountain range is home to some awe-inspiring rock formations, including the Maltese Cross and the Wolfberg Arch. In the caves and overhangs are hundreds of fascinating examples of San rock art, ranging from 300 to 6 000 years old.

Further south is the Cape Peninsula, where Cape Town sprawls between its two oceans and beneath the mountain chain running from Table Mountain to Cape Point. Cape Town's incredible natural beauty, fascinating history and architecture, Mediterranean climate, and its melting pot of peoples make it one of the world's most interesting cities. The Cape Winelands are only an hour's drive from the centre of town.

The Overberg region (literally 'over the mountain') lies over Sir Lowry's Pass as travellers leave Cape Town heading for the Garden Route. The headquarters of South Africa's apple-growing industry are the small towns of Elgin and Grabouw. On the east coast Hermanus is renowned for excellent land-based whale-watching, while nearby Gansbaai is famous for cage-diving with great white sharks. Cape Agulhas is the southernmost tip of Africa and home to South Africa's second oldest lighthouse.

Running from Mossel Bay to Storms River, the Garden Route is a scenic stretch of coastline incorporating the lushly forested mountains that rise steeply from the sea and the beautiful golden beaches that edge the shoreline.

Oudtshoorn, once the ostrich-farming capital of the world, is the main town in the Klein and Central Karoo. This sparsely populated, inland region is dotted with small towns and sheep farms; many restaurants feature 'Karoo Lamb' on their menus.

Cape Town

Affectionately nicknamed the Mother City, Cape Town has been rated one of the top destinations in the world. The city lies at the northern end of the Cape Peninsula, a 75-kilometre-long tail of mountains ending at the Cape of Good Hope Nature Reserve. Nestled at the foot of the spectacular Table Mountain – South Africa's most famous landmark – Cape Town is one of the few cities in the world that lies entirely within a national park. Drive 15 minutes in any direction and you can lose yourself in stunning landscapes of eighteenth-century Cape Dutch manors, historic wineries and white-sand beaches backed by sheer mountains.

Originally home to the nomadic Khoi people for at least 30 000 years, the Cape Peninsula was first settled in 1652 by Dutch sailors. In 1795 it became a British colony. The city was the first port of call for many European, Indian, South East Asian and Madagascan settlers. As these interspersed with the local Khoi and Xhosa, the city became a melting pot of cultures, religions, styles and flavours. Table Mountain dominates the city in a way that is difficult to imagine until you visit. The best view is from Blouberg Beach, where you can get a postcard-perfect photo of Table Mountain surrounded by the city and sparkling ocean. In the afternoon creeping fingers of clouds spill over the mountain-top creating the famous 'tablecloth'. At night the sheer cliffs are dramatically lit up for a different view. You can climb the mountain or ride the cable car to the top for some fantastic views of the city.

The city has a reputation for being the most welcoming city in South Africa. Capetonians are proud of their easygoing spirit – jokingly known as the 'Cape coma' by people in more formal Johannesburg. Capetonians also relish their social life. There are limitless restaurants, bars, nightclubs, theatres, exhibitions, flea markets and world-class shopping centres. Cape Town's restaurants offer every imaginable choice of world foods. Fresh seafood is a speciality, and there's nothing better than eating crayfish or oysters overlooking the ocean where dolphins and whales frolic. African food is well represented and there are several restaurants decked out in an African theme with game meat on the menu, often accompanied by a show of traditional dancing.

But despite its outstanding natural beauty and cosmopolitan atmosphere, Cape Town is still surrounded by the ever-visible legacy of apartheid. The first glimpse of the city coming from the airport is a stretch of rambling townships densely packed with shacks. They are a hangover from the days when the apartheid government forced the black population to live in poverty. A tour of these areas is recommended for a glimpse of the old South Africa, and to learn about the enormous challenges facing the new one. A guide, often a resident, will take you around to meet the locals and experience colourful township life. There is also the chance to have a drink and a game of pool with the locals at one of the many shebeens,

informal pubs. Another testament to apartheid is Robben Island, once the prison where Nelson Mandela was sent during his 27 years of incarceration. It is reached by a ferry that also offers outstanding views from the ocean of the city and mountain. Once on the island you are driven around in an old prison bus and then go on a guided tour of the prison that includes a glimpse of Mandela's tiny cell.

With plenty of interesting sightseeing, contemporary museums, beautiful scenery and a wide range of tours and activities, you won't be short of something to see or do in the Mother City. With a splendid national park on the doorstep and a near-perfect climate, there's a wide range of outdoor activities on offer in Cape Town: hiking, biking, sailing, fishing, surfing, diving, and more extreme adventures like abseiling, kloofing and sand-boarding. The Cape Town beaches are legendary – you can spend hours on them soaking up the sun. Some of the best beaches on the Atlantic seaboard include Clifton's First through Fourth beaches, the impossibly trendy Camps Bay and the quieter Llandudno beaches. The city centre has some fine museums including the thought-provoking District Six Museum. It tells the history of the district of Cape Town that was razed to the ground during the apartheid era because it was where whites and blacks lived together and opposed the government's ideals. The famous Victoria & Alfred Waterfront receives over 20 million visitors a year and is a must for great shopping and eating in a teeming maritime environment. From here you can take a helicopter flip over Table Mountain or a boat cruise around the harbour or beyond. There are some talented street performers; the amphitheatre often hosts live entertainment; and the Waterfront is host to a variety of craft shows and exhibitions. It's also the location of the excellent Two Oceans Aquarium. Its spectacular giant fish tanks allow you to eye a huge manta ray or a great white shark. You can even dive with the sharks if you dare.

"Cape Point is one of the greatest landmarks in the world."

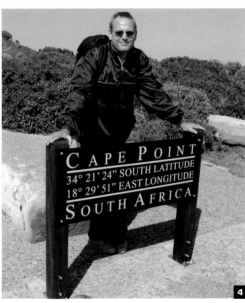

On the eastern slopes of Table Mountain you'll find Kirstenbosch National Botanical Garden. Founded in 1913, it encompasses 528 hectares of diverse and colourful indigenous plant life. On a sunny afternoon it's a wonderful spot to enjoy a lazy stroll through the cultivated gardens or head out on a hike through the surrounding fynbos and forest. Summer evenings are the perfect time to watch an outdoor concert with a picnic and a bottle of wine on the lawns.

Another must in Cape Town is a Peninsula Tour. Cape Point is one of the greatest landmarks in the world. Immerse yourself in the drama of a rugged coastline, untouched, pristine sandy beaches and hidden coves. On the way, at Hout Bay, you can take a trip out to Seal Island to see the colony of Cape fur seals, which spend their days lolling on the rocks, barking at each other or slipping into the sea for a spot of deep-sea fishing. The tour continues along the dramatic Chapman's Peak Drive where the road is literally chiselled into the mountainside. At the Cape of Good Hope Nature Reserve you can climb up to Cape Point for breathtaking views of the pounding ocean on the rocks below or hike across the rugged terrain to the peaceful beach at the Cape of Good Hope. On the way back to Cape Town there is the opportunity to visit the penguin colony at Boulders Beach where a boardwalk allows you to watch the penguins staring straight back at you.

This Spread
1 The sight of Cape Town's Table Mountain serves as a fitting end or start to any overland trip.
2 Cape of Good Hope.
3 Looking back at Cape Town from the ferry to Robben Island.
4 End of the road: Cape Point.

The Winelands

A day trip to the Cape Winelands is a fun way to explore the magnificent wine estates and raise a toast to good South African wine. The wine estates are picture-perfect country settings of mountains, valleys, lakes and historic architecture. Your guide will tell you something about the different types of wine and fermenting processes, and you'll have the chance to sample some locally produced wines, such as Pinotage and Shiraz, in wonderful garden surroundings.

Considered by many to be the heart of the South African wine industry, the Stellenbosch area incorporates 106 cellars, many of which are open to the public for tours and wine-tasting. Wander down oak-lined Dorp Street in the heart of Stellenbosch and soak up the historic atmosphere of this university town. Several hiking- and mountain-biking trails lie in the surrounding mountains. Best enjoyed in the autumn or spring is the 24-kilometre Vineyard Trail, which winds through vineyards, olive groves and forest plantations. In the nearby Jonkershoek Nature Reserve you'll find a number of hikes ranging in length and degree of difficulty.

Lying 30 kilometres east of Stellenbosch is the picturesque town of Franschhoek. Its name literally means 'French corner' in reference to the Huguenot refugees who settled there in 1688. Today Franschhoek is a thriving little town that's celebrated for its fine wine and superb cuisine. Hiking, fishing and hang-gliding are all on offer in the valley.

"...a toast to good wine..."

Paarl (Dutch for 'pearl') is dominated by the three massive, rounded granite outcrops that form Paarl Mountain, one of the largest solid rocks in the world. Located 56 kilometres from Cape Town this quaint town offers the chance to enjoy some of the area's architectural heritage, historic charm and natural beauty. For the energetic visitor there are hiking and cycling trails, while the local wine estates offer tastings, tours and food. Two of the more famous wineries in the local area are KWV and Nederburg.

Whale-watching

On the northern shore of Walker Bay, Hermanus was founded as a fishing village in 1855 and is now a popular holiday resort. Walker Bay is renowned as a playground of the southern right whale. These marine giants arrive in May to calve, raise their young and mate. Prime whale-spotting months are August until November. The 12-kilometre Cliff Path that hugs the shoreline offers superb opportunities for land-based whale-watching, allowing uninterrupted views of the whales as they bask in the coves below. Watch out for the whale crier with his unusual kelp horn and sandwich board, which announces the day's best sightings.

Shark-diving

Half an hour's drive east of Hermanus is the small fishing village of Gansbaai (Goose Bay), which over recent years has become the great white shark capital of the world. Twelve kilometres off the coast lie Dyer and Geyser islands; the stretch of water between these is known as 'Shark Alley'.

Pages 270-271
A Cape Dutch wine farm in the shadow of Table Mountain.

This Spread
1 The wine farms around Stellenbosch, Paarl and Franschhoek lie in picturesque valleys surrounded by craggy peaks.
2 Many of the homesteads on the wine estates are original Cape Dutch manor houses.
3 Diving with great white sharks is a memorable experience.

That's because the islands are home to 30 000 Cape fur seals, the preferred meal of the great white shark. Also helping the shark population to flourish is the fact that these mammals are protected by South African law. Every day boats head out to Shark Alley where the sharks are lured with bait, then a steel cage attached to the boat is lowered into the sea. Sharks come within a couple of metres of the boats and cages, and it's a truly memorable experience to be in the water with one of nature's most efficient predators.

Garden Route

The Garden Route runs along a scenic stretch of coastline beginning in Cape Town and ending in Port Elizabeth and is a string of attractive towns, beaches, oyster-rich lagoons and dense forests. The region has become South Africa's most popular tourist destination after Cape Town, and it's not hard to see why. Visitors are drawn year-round to its indigenous forests, freshwater lakes, wetlands, hidden coves and long beaches. The Garden Route is also bordered by impressive mountain ranges, and the interior is reached via a number of magnificent passes that take you to the wide open spaces of the Karoo. The towns occupy idyllic locations overlooking swathes of beaches or rocky coastline, and places like Mossel Bay, Wilderness, Knysna, and Plettenberg Bay are well-developed tourist resorts. Each has a variety of holiday accommodation, souvenir shops, museums, and restaurants and bars. The Garden

Route also features a range of adventure activities, including the mother of all bungee jumps at Bloukrans Bridge – the highest commercial jump in the world. You can also go black-water tubing at Storms River Mouth, go cage-diving with a great white shark, or climb on the back of an ostrich in Oudtshoorn.

Tsitsikamma National Park

At the eastern end of the Garden Route, on a rocky coastline with cliffs that press close to the sea is the Tsitsikamma National Park. This is a place of awe-inspiring beauty, where the booming breakers of the Indian Ocean relentlessly pound rocky shores. Tsitsikamma (pronounced sit-si-kama) is a Khoisan word meaning, 'place of much water'. With an abundance of rivers and streams running through sandstone gorges, it's a fitting name. The park incorporates an 80-kilometre stretch of coastline of deep forests and secluded valleys, and the park boundary extends five kilometres into the ocean to protect the inter-tidal, reef and deep-sea ecosystems where dolphins and whales swim. When it was proclaimed in 1964, it became the first Marine National Park in Africa. The terrestrial portion of park is home to the rare Cape clawless otter, vervet monkeys and baboons, and the forests hide small antelopes including the blue duiker.

Scuba diving, snorkelling and canoeing are all on offer in the park. It's also a hiker's paradise. Two well-established hikes are run by the National

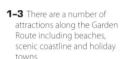

1–3 There are a number of attractions along the Garden Route including beaches, scenic coastline and holiday towns.
4 Bloukrans Bridge east of Plettenberg Bay.
5 The entire Cape Peninsula, Overberg and Garden Route are characterised by beautiful bays with sandy beaches.
6 The bungee jump from Bloukrans Bridge on the Garden Route is the highest in the world at 216 metres.

"...awe-inspiring beauty where booming breakers pound rocky shores..."

Parks Board. The 72-kilometre Tsitsikamma Trail winds through the mountains, while the 5-day Otter Trail hugs the coast from Storms River Mouth to the estuary at Nature's Valley. Both trails require a reasonable level of fitness and must be booked at least a year in advance, so forward planning's needed if you want to experience either one. There are also a number of short walking trails, one of which crosses a wobbly suspension bridge.

Bungee jumping

South Africa is home to the highest commercial bungee jump in the world. At 216 metres, this jump's first rebound is longer than the full descent at Victoria Falls. It's on the Garden Route at the Bloukrans Bridge, which marks the border between the Eastern Cape and Western Cape provinces. There are also a range of jumps and a bridge swing on the much lower Gourits River Bridge, also on the Garden Route closer to Cape Town.

Pages 276–267
The lush green canopy of Tsitsikamma's last remaining indigenous forest.

This Spread
1&2 Elephants at Addo Elephant National Park. Here you are almost guaranteed good sightings of the many herds of elephants.

Eastern Cape

The coast of the Eastern Cape is dominated by sweeping uncluttered beaches, exotic river mouths and hidden coves. The famous Wild Coast remains just that – wild, untamed and naturally preserved. The hills are topped with Xhosa villages and farms where the way of life hasn't changed for hundreds of years, and the scenes are more reminiscent of rural Tanzania or Kenya than any other part of South Africa. It's a great place to meet the local villagers or take a lonely stroll on an endless and empty beach.

Addo Elephant National Park

The Eastern Cape is also home to the excellent Addo Elephant National Park, located an hour's drive from Port Elizabeth. The park has recently been extended and now covers 370 000 hectares of terrestrial park and 120 000 hectares of marine territory. Lion have recently been reintroduced to the park and it's now possible to see the Big Seven here – lion, rhino, buffalo, leopard, elephant, shark and whale. It was proclaimed a game reserve in 1931 to safeguard, from hunters, the last remaining 11 wild elephants that were still roaming the area. Since then the herds have grown steadily,

and today Addo contains over 350 elephants. It's fascinating to watch them emerge from dense tangles of creepers and trees and guide their young towards the waterholes. The giant dung beetle is also an important occupant of this park. A few facts about an elephant's digestive system help demonstrate why: an adult elephant deposits around 150 kilograms of dung every day, dispatched every 15 minutes. The dung beetle has an enormous job clearing up. The flightless dung beetle is found exclusively in this park (other dung beetles can fly), and are important to the ecology of the area. No citrus fruits can be taken into the park as Addo elephants have developed a craving for them. The mere whiff of an orange sends them into a frenzy!

The easiest way to explore the park is by car; there are 75 kilometres of road and several lookout points at waterholes where animals gather. Guided game drives are also available. For those who prefer being on foot, guided hikes in search of rhino and elephant are a fantastic way to get a close-up look at these large mammals. A variety of horse-riding trails are also on offer for both inexperienced and more capable riders. There's an illuminated waterhole at the main rest-camp for night-time game-viewing.

Jeffreys Bay

This seaside town, 72 kilometres west of Port Elizabeth, is home to southern Africa's most famous waves. J-Bay, as it's known to surfers the world over, is a 'right-hand point break' that includes sections such as 'supertubes' and 'boneyards'. When good conditions – the necessary tide, wind- and swell direction – prevail, all the sections begin to join up to produce a perfectly formed wave that gives surfers one of the longest rides in the world. The Billabong Surfing Festival is held in July every year, as it's during the winter months that the largest swells arrive. It's not unheard of to find some of J-Bay's original surfers – dolphins – playing in the waves alongside the board-riders.

2

KwaZulu-Natal

KwaZulu-Natal is one South Africa's largest provinces. It lies south of Mozambique in the east of the country. A fair-size chunk of the balmy Indian Ocean coastline falls within this province. Durban is the province's main city and transport hub. To the north of Durban, the rocky valleys and rural hills of Zululand have some superb national parks, notably Hluhluwe-Imfolozi. This park is best known for its successful 'Operation Rhino', which brought the white rhino back from the brink of extinction. It's an unusual park in that it's hilly, making for great viewing of the Big Five. The Greater St Lucia Wetland Park is the third largest wilderness area in the country. It was declared a World Heritage Site for its important eco-systems. The lake itself teems with crocodiles, and sharks bask in the estuary mouth. It's one of the only places in the world where crocs and sharks share the same water. There are some pristine beaches at Cape Vidal and at Sodwana Bay, also the country's most popular spot for scuba diving. Further north, Maputuland's game sanctuaries epitomise the best of the African wilderness, and there are some unique and peaceful wetland reserves. The habitat here ranges from coastal dune forests to open bushveld and supports a wide diversity of game and birdlife.

Between the coastal playground and the majestic Drakensberg Mountains is a region of gentle pastoral beauty known as the Midlands. Plump cows graze on the battlefields of the Zulu and Anglo-Boer wars. The most violent battle occurred when the Zulu leader, Shaka, murdered the Boer leader, Piet Retief, sending the settlers into a panic. In December 1838 the Zulus were badly defeated at the terrible Battle of Blood River, where thousands of Zulus died due to the Boers' overwhelming firepower. The river turned deep red with their blood.

Durban

San hunter-gatherers walked its beaches; European sailors anchored in the bay called Rio de Natal by Vasco da Gama in 1497; British settlers endured a precarious existence in what was then a small harbour town; conflict between the Voortrekkers, English and Zulus was common in the nineteenth century; Indian settlers arrived here 100 years ago to work on Natal's sugar plantations. Now home to more than three million people, Durban is a fragrant city with an exotic blend of many cultures. The mosque is the biggest in the southern hemisphere, and there are some interesting Indian markets and bazaars. Durban is where you will find the famous Durban curry which can be sampled at a number of excellent restaurants.

There's a strip of holiday development in the city and on the beaches to the north and south. Durban's neon-lit Golden Mile has high-rise holiday flats, aquariums and water parks. The subtropical climate and warm waters of the Indian Ocean have made it a mecca for seaside pursuits. Beach culture reigns here; it's a great spot for bathing and surfing.

uKhahlamba-Drakensberg National Park

Snow-capped in winter, the uKhahlamba-Drakensberg National Park is the country's grandest mountain range and another World Heritage Site. The park runs for hundreds of kilometres down the eastern border of the kingdom of Lesotho, a small mountainous country completely surrounded by South Africa. The mountain range is known to the Zulu people as 'Quathlamba' – the 'barrier of spears'. The peaks, reaching higher than 3 000 metres, have names like Giant's Castle, Cathedral Peak and Bushmen's Nek.

"exotic blend of cultures"

As you'd expect in such a breath-taking landscape, the possibilities for outdoor adventure are endless. Hiking trails, ranging from a leisurely walk lasting for only a few hours to much more strenuous multi-day excursions, traverse the park. Horse-riding and mountain-biking trails are also on offer. If you'd rather get a bird's-eye view of these peaks and valleys, this is a fantastic place for hang-gliding, micro-lighting and paragliding, so contact a local flying club. Mountain climbing, abseiling and ice climbing are all popular Drakensberg activities, but it's wise to undertake any of these in the company of an experienced

mountaineer who's familiar with the area. Fast-flowing rivers are frequented by anglers hoping for a record-breaking rainbow trout. The less energetic can just drink in the birdsong, the crisp clean air and the stunning views.

Scuba diving

Thanks to the warm Agulhas current flowing down the KwaZulu-Natal coast, the water temperature seldom falls below 20 degrees Celsius, allowing colourful tropical reefs to thrive. This has made the coastline one of South Africa's premier diving locations.

Only four hours' drive from Durban, Sodwana Bay is the province's most popular dive site. Although it's diveable year-round, the best conditions are from November until May. The Sodwana Bay reefs are named after their distance from the launch site, with 7 Mile generally considered the most impressive. More than 1 200 fish species have been identified here, and a sighting of migrating ragged tooth sharks can almost be guaranteed from July until November.

Lying off the small coastal town of Umkomaas, 40 minutes south of Durban, you'll find Aliwal Shoal, a fossilised sand dune that lies five kilometres offshore. A variety of hard and soft corals, and the convergence of reef- and cold-water fish make this an interesting dive site. You can also dive off the Produce, a Norwegian freighter that struck the shoal and sank in 1974; it now rests in 30 metres of water.

If you're keen to see pelagic fish and larger sharks, then a dive at Protea Banks is worthwhile. This deep-water adventure happens eight kilometres offshore at Shelly Beach, south of Port Shepstone. This dive commences at 25 metres, and participants often spot Zambezi, hammerhead and tiger sharks during summer, and ragged tooth sharks in the winter months.

1 Shark-infested waters at uShaka Marine World, Durban.
2 Beachfront Durban.
3 Camping in the Drakensberg mountains.
4 Rhino in Hluhluwe-Imfolozi.
5 The uKhahlamba-Drakensberg National Park has been declared a World Heritage Site for its natural beauty.

Pages 284–285
Cathedral Peak Camp in uKhahlamba-Drakensberg National Park.

Mpumalanga

Mpumalanga is one of South Africa's most visited destinations, thanks to its magnificent scenery, flora and fauna and the saga of the 1870s gold rush. The province is in the north-eastern part of South Africa. It is bordered by Mozambique to the east and the Kingdom of Swaziland to the south and east. This is where the foothills of the Drakensberg lead on to the endless game plains of the Greater Kruger National Park. Next to Kruger is the wonderfully green Blyde River Canyon. It's the third largest in the world, after the Grand and Fish River, and has 700-metre cliffs that support dams and waterfalls. This area is frequently referred to as the Panorama Region and for good reason. It has some impressive mountains, lofty passes, dramatic valleys, rivers and forests. There are some fabulous viewpoints at the top of the canyon and a tremendous view from 'God's Window' to Kruger and beyond to Mozambique, across the hot lowveld at the bottom of the canyon. Also

at the top, where the Treur and the Blyde rivers meet, are the Bourke's Luck Potholes which are worth a stop: a natural feature of rocks hewn over centuries by the movement of water.

The entire area offers great opportunities for adventure, from simple bird-watching, to hiking, horse-riding and fishing. Rivers once panned for gold can now be enjoyed on a vibrant white-water trip, and the forests where prospectors once camped can be explored by quad-bike. Just outside Graskop, on the lip of an escarpment, is an exciting gorge swing and flying fox – the sister operation to the one at Victoria Falls. The quaint Panorama towns at the top of the canyon are home to tearooms and shops selling homemade jam and patchwork-quilts. Graskop is a picturesque town surrounded by waterfalls. It is famous for its excellent pancake cafes. Sabie is an important forestry centre. The hills are covered in pine plantations, creating one of the largest man-made forests in the world. Steeped in the history of pioneers, hunters

and fortune seekers, there are some fascinating gold rush towns such as Barberton and Pilgrim's Rest. The latter is the only village in South Africa that is a National Monument. The quaint Victorian cottages have been fully restored. It's possible to try your luck at gold panning, and even venture down a 100-year-old mine at Barberton.

Greater Kruger National Park

The Greater Kruger National Park covers a significant chunk of South Africa – from the Crocodile River in Mpumalanga in the south to the Zimbabwe border in the Limpopo Province in the north. On its entire eastern side is the border with Mozambique. Recently there has been progress in extending this wilderness region as part of a trans-frontier park with Zimbabwe and Mozambique. The fences along borders and those between the private game reserves on the fringes of Kruger have been taken down now to form the Greater Kruger National Park, creating what could

possibly be the most game-rich piece of land in the world. This gives the animals a much larger area within which to migrate, and Kruger is now around 24 000 square kilometres, or roughly the size of Israel. Its density of permanent game is

1 Blyde River Canyon.
2 Guinea fowl.
3 Zebra.
4 Cheetah.

> "It's a fantastic chance to have a more personal encounter with nature and to discover the smaller creatures that can easily be overlooked from a moving vehicle."

unrivalled by any other park in Africa, and there are hundreds of different species of birds, mammals, reptiles, fish and amphibians.

The park was first proclaimed in 1898 as the Sabie Game Reserve by Paul Kruger, then president of the Transvaal Republic. The first motorists entered the park in 1927 for a fee of one British Pound. Since then Kruger has received hundreds of thousands of visitors each year and the park has superb facilities, with an excellent network of roads and game-viewing waterholes. The camps have every amenity, from shops to banks to laundromats, and can accommodate up to 5 000 people per day. Then there are the many luxury camps in the private reserves where people's game experiences are complemented by plush facilities with swimming pools, beauty spas and sumptuous food and accommodation. Occasionally it gets crowded, with many vehicles parked around the same pride of lion. But with a 2 600-kilometre road network there are plenty of opportunities to go out into the bush.

Wilderness Hiking Trails

Strange as it may sound, it's possible to hike in Kruger. Wilderness Trails are conducted by an experienced, armed game ranger who guides a group of eight people through parts of the park that can best be explored on foot. It's a fantastic chance to have a more personal encounter with nature and to discover the smaller creatures that can easily be overlooked from a moving vehicle. Five established trails take place in different parts of the park, each with its own unique attractions – one area is rich in San paintings, another passes a year-round waterhole where animals gather, while another traverses an area known for its prolific birdlife. Trails last for three days and are run from mid-February to mid-December, but they are in high demand so make a reservation at least twelve months ahead.

Mountain biking

Guided mountain-bike trails were introduced in Kruger in 2003, allowing visitors access to pristine parts of the park that are rarely seen. For safety reasons only riders over the age of 16 can participate, and all groups are accompanied by experienced field guides. Three return trails of varying lengths are currently on offer. All routes depart from Oliphants Camp and follow jeep tracks and game paths. Good-quality equipment

Pages 288–289
Blyde River Canyon
in Mpumalanga.

can be rented at the camp, though riders may provide their own gear which must include a puncture repair kit – a hint that thorn trees are plentiful. The rides range in classification from easy to difficult, so all skill levels are catered for. Mountain biking through the park is an unforgettable way to experience the incredible wealth of animal- and birdlife that makes this park home.

Gauteng

Gauteng is South Africa's smallest and wealthiest province. It is built on the fortunes of the gold that has been mined here for over 100 years. In 1886, on a patch of windswept grassland, an unemployed miner stumbled upon a stone bearing traces of gold. Speculators, prospectors, fortune-seekers and adventurers arrived in the area from all over the world. Gold rush shantytowns sprang up and were rapidly transformed into modern concrete cities; Johannesburg became 'The Gold Capital of the World', and the entire country was catapulted into an economic boom.

Today Gauteng (meaning 'place of gold' in Sesotho) largely consists of the two principle cities Johannesburg and Pretoria. They are 50 kilometres apart but these days are practically joined by a ribbon of development and the N1 freeway. Pretoria is the judicial capital of the country, whilst Johannesburg is the financial capital and an important hub for air travel.

Johannesburg

This city warrants a couple of days of exploration, and there are some interesting and informative tours on offer. There's a vibrant restaurant, live music and clubbing scene, and the shopping in the giant malls is definitely worth making time for. No visitor should miss the theme park at Gold Reef City and the excellent Apartheid Museum next to the mine museum. Constitution Hill, on the site of the original fort and prison, is another extraordinarily powerful museum and tourist attraction that aims to give visitors an experi-

ence of the stark realities of life during the harsh and repressive days of apartheid. Through unique creativity and inspired design, the architecture and displays are graphic, unsettling and thought-provoking, and yet uplifting.

Jo'burg's twin city, populated exclusively by black people, is Soweto (an acronym for South-western Townships). The type of housing ranges from shacks to large mansions. In one street you can find the houses of two Nobel Peace Prize winners: Nelson Mandela and Archbishop Desmond Tutu. Also located in Soweto is the Baragwanath Hospital, thought to be the largest hospital in the southern hemisphere. It was in Soweto that much of the struggle against apartheid was fought. It's a good idea to go on a tour, which often includes a visit to Nelson Mandela's former home (now a museum); the various monuments erected to commemorate moments in the history of the struggle; and a shebeen, a traditional township pub.

Pretoria

Pretoria is a more placid city and lacks the vibe of Johannesburg. Numbers of Voortrekkers arrived in the region in the 1850s. An air of history pervades much of central Pretoria, especially Church Square around which the city grew. The square was the site of the first church, the first markets and the first shops. Here you'll find the old monuments, government buildings and courthouses associated with the apartheid era.

Pretoria has over a hundred parks and is renowned for its colourful gardens, shrubs and trees; it's particularly beautiful in spring when jacarandas envelop the avenues in mauve. Some points of interest in Pretoria are the Voortrekker Monument, a striking memorial built to honour the early pioneers; the Kruger House Museum; and Church Square in the centre of the city, where the statue of Paul Kruger looks down on the passers by. The imposing Union Buildings, which house the office of the president, provide an impressive view over the city.

This Spread
1 Lion.
2 Johannesburg city centre.
3 Union Buildings, Pretoria.

Pages 292–293
Greater Kruger National Park could be the most game-rich land in the world.

PHOTO CREDITS

Acacia Africa: p15, 20, 73, 115, 148, 165. **Adrift:** p80. **Africa Travel Co:** back cover, 21, 30, 40, 56, 57, 72, 83, 85, 112, 114, 123, 125, 132, 142, 155, 201, 206, 220, 221, 226, 228, 245, 250, 251, 290. **African Routes:** p10, 14, 18, 21, 28, 31, 47, 56, 59, 108, 109, 112, 115, 118, 145, 151, 154, 166, 187, 193, 197, 207, 225, 244, 249, 266, 275, 278. **All Terrain Adventures:** p79. **Alter Action:** p240, 241. **Andrew Bannister (Images of Africa):** p51, 54, 60, 64, 68, 69. **Arnold & Alicia Estrada:** p15, 25, 39, 53, 56. **Arnout Hemel & Saskia de Jongh:** p14, 23, 32, 38, 50, 65, 83, 200, 254, 273. **Chanan Weiss (Images of Africa):** p120. **Coen & Jeanette Zijlstra:** p13, 14, 22, 23, 25, 27, 53, 56, 59, 70, 73, 74, 75, 80, 82, 83, 84, 85, 90, 91, 92, 93, 132, 134, 182, 185, 190, 193, 203, 206, 207, 213, 215, 222, 224, 225, 228, 244, 247, 249, 250, 254, 257, 260, 263, 266, 267, 268, 269, 272, 286. **Darren Humphrys:** back cover, 20, 30, 31, 36, 43, 56, 58, 59, 73, 74, 76, 77, 86, 88, 89, 95, 97, 100, 105, 108, 112, 123, 124, 129, 132, 139, 143, 149, 151, 184, 185, 208, 210, 225, 229, 233, 234, 244, 248, 251, 279. **Daryl & Sharna Balfour (Images of Africa):** p51, 66, 68, 69. **Evan Haussmann:** p8, 12, 29, 134, 247, 252. **Francesco Dicorato:** p19, 43, 46, 59, 61, 64, 72, 73, 77, 83, 85, 88, 96, 97, 100, 187, 201, 209, 212, 213. **Gerhard Dreyer (Images of Africa):** p274, 276. **Ground Rush Adventures:** p239. **Hein von Hörsten (Images of Africa):** p274. **Helen Patchette:** p2, 168, 185, 186, 190, 191. **John Robinson:** p282. **Ian Michler (Images of Africa):** p136. **Karibu Safaris:** p21, 203, 221. **Keith Begg (Images of Africa):** p152, 172, 188. **Kobus Lubbe:** p274, 275. **Kumuka:** back cover, 19, 28, 43, 52, 57, 61, 89, 112, 114, 118, 135, 166. **Lanz von Hörsten:** p282. **Lizzie Williams:** p62, 63, 64, 75, 81, 83, 101, 108, 109, 112, 116, 117, 118, 123, 124, 127, 128, 129, 134, 150, 151, 153, 174, 175, 180, 191, 201, 221, 224, 225, 233, 237, 238, 243, 254, 269, 272, 273, 287. **Mario Travaini:** back cover, 26, 45, 48, 98, 102, 106, 110, 130, 140, 171, 194, 198, 216, 258. **Michael Poliza:** p226, 227, 229, 232 **Nigel J Dennis (Images of Africa):** p204, 292. **Oasis Overland:** back cover, 10, 12, 13, 14, 19, 21, 29, 31, 33, 36, 37, 38, 40, 41, 50, 59, 60, 70, 74, 78, 89, 101, 104, 118, 132, 142, 145, 150, 187, 193, 220, 222, 224, 233, 236, 243, 244, 245, 247, 250, 263. **Outback Orange:** p241, 242. **Paul Goldstein/Exodus:** front cover, back cover, 147, 197, 215, 219, 246, 262. **Peter Blackwell (Images of Africa):** p16, 34, 58, 104, 113, 114, 125, 126, 128, 248. **Peter Pickford (Images of Africa):** p230, 286. **Peter Ribton (Images of Africa):** p104, 135, 143. **Phoenix Expeditions:** p31, 182, 202, 228, 287. **Roger De La Harpe (Images of Africa):** p176, 185, 191, 280, 283. **Safari Par Excellence:** p162, 163, 168, 174, 175. **Shaen Adey (Images of Africa):** p264, 270, 283, 284. **Shearwater:** back cover, 145, 146, 147, 162, 163, 166, 169, 179, 180, 181, 182. **Steven Derungs:** p23, 38, 40, 178, 181, 227. **Tanzania Tourism:** p109. **Wagon Trails:** p203. **Walter Knirr (Images of Africa):** p283, 291, 288. **Wild Horizons:** p145, 152, 154, 158, 160, 161, 164.

www.imagesofafrica.co.za

IMAGES OF AFRICA
P H O T O   L I B R A R Y

INDEX

Page numbers in *italics* indicate illustrations.

ACKNOWLEDGEMENTS

Thanks to the many commercial overland companies, truck crew, passengers and independent overlanders whose photographs are featured in this book, ensuring that in every way it is a memento by those who have been-there, done-that. I hope you will enjoy seeing them used in this record of your journey. The independent overlanders who had the privilege of driving, riding or cycling from one end of Africa to the other are: Steven Derungs (*www. contrast.cx*); Arnold & Alicia Estrada (*www. aandagotoafrica.com*); Arnout Hemel & Saskia de Jongh (*www.arnoutensaskia.com*); Coen & Jeanette Zijlstra (*www.in.2-africa.nl*); Dirk Louwers (*www.vtv1.nl/adriveforwildlife*); David & Katja Horner (*www.duksjourney.net*); David Priddis (*www.walkabout2408.com*); Scotty Robinson (*www.offbeatroads. com*); Andy and Clare Lees (*www.kusafiri.net*); and Mario Travaini (*www.southing.com*).

Truck passengers and crew include myself; Darren Humphrys; Leanne Guild; Helen Patchett (*www. safarisouth.co.zw*); Francesco Dicorato and Glenn Annetts.

The overland companies that contributed were Oasis Overland (*www.oasisoverland.co.uk*); Kumuka Expeditions (*www.kumuka.com*); Exodus (*www.exodus.co.uk*); Phoenix Expeditions (*www. phoenixexpeditions.co.uk*); Africa Travel Co. (*www.africatravelco.com*); Acacia Africa (*www.acacia-africa.com*); Karibu & Kiboko Safaris (*www.karibu.co.za, www.kiboko.co.za*); African Routes (*www. africanroutes.co.za*); Wildlife Adventures (*www.wildlifeadventures.co.za*); African in Focus (*www. africa-in-focus.com*).

Activities operators that contributed images were, in Zimbabwe and Zambia: Safari Par Excellence (*www.safpar.com*); Shearwater Adventures (*www.shearwateradventures.com*); Wild Horizons (*www. wildhorizons.co.zw*). In Uganda: All Terrain Adventures (*www.traveluganda.co.ug*). In Namibia: Outback Orange (*www.hansahotel.com.na/outback_orange.htm*); Alter Action Sand Boarding (*www. alter-action.com*); and Ground Rush Adventures (*www.africa-adventure.org/g/groundrush*). In South Africa: Kobus Lubbe and Face Adrenalin (*www.faceadrenalin.com*).

For more information about overlanding and overland tours visit *www.overlandafrica.com*. (I am also the author of this site – the leading website on travelling overland through eastern and southern Africa.)